James L. Jordan was stationed in Bangkok, Thailand, during the Vietnam War. And immediately after being released from the army, he migrated to the San Francisco area, where he participated in one of the last civil rights marches of the 1960s. Disillusioned by how little has changed over the years in civil rights arena, he wrote this book to show how major a role the black folks have played in sabotaging the upward mobility of their own race. He has written three other books: *It's a Weird! Weird! World!!* And, *Work from Home Recycling Big Money Products.* And he is currently working on a sequel to *Plantation Negroes of the 21st Century.*

To my grandson, Ethan

James L. Jordan

PLANTATION NEGROES OF THE 21ˢᵗ CENTURY

AUSTIN MACAULEY PUBLISHERS™

LONDON • CAMBRIDGE • NEW YORK • SHARJAH

Copyright © James L. Jordan 2024

All rights reserved. No part of this publication may be reproduced, distributed, or transmitted in any form or by any means, including photocopying, recording, or other electronic or mechanical methods, without the prior written permission of the publisher, except in the case of brief quotations embodied in critical reviews and certain other non-commercial uses permitted by copyright law. For permission requests, write to the publisher.

Any person who commits any unauthorized act in relation to this publication may be liable for criminal prosecution and civil claims for damages.

The story, experiences, and words are the author's alone.

Ordering Information
Quantity sales: Special discounts are available on quantity purchases by corporations, associations, and others. For details, contact the publisher at the address below.

Publisher's Cataloging-in-Publication data
Jordan, James L.
Plantation Negroes of the 21st Century

ISBN 9798886937275 (Paperback)
ISBN 9798886937282 (ePub e-book)

Library of Congress Control Number: 2023921554

www.austinmacauley.com/us

First Published 2024
Austin Macauley Publishers LLC
40 Wall Street, 33rd Floor, Suite 3302
New York, NY 10005
USA

mail-usa@austinmacauley.com
+1 (646) 5125767

All that I am or will ever be… I owe to my mother, Miss Evelina,
whose light is sorely missed.

Table of Contents

Introduction

Has the Black race been ostracized into a purgatory world, where it is neither free nor enslaved, and where the landscape looks remarkably like the Old Plantation?

Dr. Claud Anderson, former Assistant Secretary of Commerce, says: "Black folks in proportional comparative terms are regressing. Blacks have been socially engineered into the lowest levels of life… and are now more hated than at any time in the last fifty years."

Dr. Anderson does not come right out and say, that Blacks are still stationed, near the Old Plantation, but he comes awfully close.

And how sweet it would be, if we could blame the devil white man for keeping poor helpless Black folks chained, to oppression, oh the tears we could shed for all the blood and sweat and tears the white man has inflicted on God's po' Black chilluns, oh mercy, mercy, mercy!

But: the plain fact of the matter is, that that road that has led the Black race here to this perilous moment in time leads us back to a host of villains: the white ones, we all know about; the Black ones (*Negroes*, who exploit their fellow sufferers) we conveniently choose to forget about.

Black folks should know that their *friends*, and their *enemies*… are not always who they *appear* to be.

This book will be a journey: A journey that begins in 1865. It will end in the turbulent 21st century.

We will travel the roads the freed slaves walked when they were loosed from horrors of slavery.

And walking in the shoes of those Old-Time slaves we will observe their horrific history. And as we travel in their foot-steps, we will be searching the landscape to get a clearer, more accurate picture, of the man-made—and *natural* impediments—that hindered their progress.

And if it is true that Black folks remain in a sort of purgatory world, where they are neither free nor enslaved, were there (and are there now) sinister forces at work, behind the scenes, to keep Ol Massa's former slaves in a permanent state of servitude?

And, more troubling, could there be, black, sinister forces at work, behind the scenes, aiding and abetting their white allies; to keep their Black brothers and sisters down and *knocked* totally *out*, on this *new* but very *old*, plantation?

Along this trail of tears, we will witness those moments in history, *when* things went wrong, *where* they went wrong, *how* they went wrong, *why* they went wrong, and we will name names along the way.

And when this journey delivers us to the present moment, perhaps we will know, *why*, the Black race is *still…* stationed… so *close…* to the Old Plantation.

Chapter One
Free at Last!

The year is 1865.

And the Black slaves are free... FREE at last! They are free—from the chain! Free—from the whip! Free—from back-breaking subjugation! Free—to be their own masters!

Yes. They are free.

But in their wild excitement, certain, nagging questions, are beginning to sober them up, and bring them around to a suddenly terrifying reality: and now whispered questions are heard circulating quietly, but urgently, amongst some of the wiser old slaves, who are very intimately aware of their old master's iron-willed desire to keep them down and out on the Old Plantation.

And if their former masters *had* miraculously decided to let bygone be bygones and allow his very valuable property to simply walk away unmolested: Where would they shelter themselves...? How would they provide food for their families...? And, more frighteningly, could they *survive*, among a deeply resentful people, who had only recently been their masters and their mistresses?

On paper they appear to be free, free to come and go as they please... But, *something*... is in the air, a kind of coldness, and an unnerving, sneaky suspicion, that *something*... is not right... There have been bloody signs along the roads; black bodies lying in ditches, their throats cut by machetes; bloody places along the trails have shown scenes of brutal battles; scenes where Black fathers had died swinging clubs and axe-handles, where mothers had fallen shielding babies; and there have even been sightings of charred black bodies that were lynched, set on fire, and viciously mutilated.

And now… as we and the freed slaves at our sides stick to the woods, avoiding white faces, and the white towns, as much as possible, we are acutely aware of any change in the wind; the faintest snapping of a twig elicits panic among the children traveling with us.

And as we pick our way carefully through the woods, we are left to naïvely wonder:

Can the savagery behind these atrocities that we have witnessed be blamed solely on the color of our skin? Are these attacks the work of a few angry townspeople; or could Ol Massa be up to his old tricks; his old corralling the Negro back onto the old plantation kind of tricks?

Those horrific scenes: were they *warnings*; gory, bloody signs, warning the former slave that he should remain close, skin close, to his benevolent former masters?

Our walk upon this dangerous road toward freedom continues: And almost overnight there seems to be more and more restrictions confronting us, more and more places that are now off limits to us…

We have all walked so far, and those alongside of us have grown feeble, and old; and as they pause, and gaze around at the never-ending, unchanging landscape, we see in their dark, withered faces, an etched, deeply ingrained sense of hopelessness.

And that, *coldness*, and that same, unnerving, sneaky suspicions that were felt soon after slavery, are *still* with us, only, *colder*, and much more *restrictive*, and much more *threatening*:

And the Old-Time slaves, alongside of us, who have walked so far, and for *so* long, are beginning to suspect that they were never meant to be free; that they were brought here as slaves and as a slaves they are destined to live out their last few years—beholding to the white man for even the air that they breathe; and in their faces is a sad awareness, that for them, nothing, will *ever* change: They seem to *know*, without doubt, that for them, and, for their descendants an invisible road has been paved in front of them, that only leads from one plantation, to the next, into infinity.

But, still, we walk on:

And the years fade into decades… the decades into a half century…

And we notice that many of those Old Timers who began the journey with us have gone to Glory, or have grown far too old to continue the walk—to freedom: We have been Ku Klux Klan terrorized, and in some cases outright genocided, and we have been railroaded onto chain-gangs, and Black Coded into a kind of second-class citizenship that looks very much like slavery, without the chains…

But miraculously, in the cold threatening night, we have stumbled, dazed, and confused… into the roaring 1930s! And glory be! We see a lighted… Wonderland!

But… as we pause… and gawk at the bright gaudy neon signs and the fresh but unchanged surroundings; we are struck with a jarring, disturbing reality: The Black race is as hated, and as disadvantaged, and as vulnerable to injustice as it was during, and soon after, slavery.

And with wide-eyed amazement, we see that we have taken only a few, tiny, baby steps… from the Massa's old, plantation.

"I don't see the younger Negroes are doing any better than we did. Though they are free, and have schools, their present condition here is mighty bad."

—Lincoln Watkins, former slave; interviewed by the WPA in the 1930s.

We have now traveled well into the 1930s… and we notice, that… *coldness*… is still there; still *there*… in the air.

And as quickly as switching on a light bulb we have jettisoned into the turbulent 1960s… And we find ourselves dodging smoke bombs on a bridge in Selma Alabama.

Snarling dogs are snapping viciously at our faces. We *feel* the body-numbing police batons thudding into our blind, reeling eyes. We *see* a white policeman riding a Black mother to the ground in a choke-hold, and that… *coldness*… is painfully *felt*, in the *air*.

And it *feels* as if… precious little has changed.

And suddenly… we have broken the sound barrier; and we are now jetting into the year 2023.

And as we alight on solid ground and settle back and catch our collective breath, we glance out the sooty window of our hot, smoking time-machine… and what in the world is the first thing that we see?

A Black race that is just as hated, as disadvantaged, and as vulnerable to injustice, as ever. A Black race with some very *close* relations, to their Ol' Massa's *former plantation.*

And that *coldness*, in the air, is *still* there; and it *seems* as if, as if… it might be there—forever.

"The Constitution," says former Assistant Secretary of Commerce, Claud Anderson, "was written for white people… When the Founding Fathers met in Philadelphia to craft the Constitution, they spent two days debating how they would write a constitution that would exclude only slaves. They came up with a Constitution that said all people shall have [certain rights]. But when you see the term 'all people', they were talking about white people. When talking about Blacks, they said things like, those in servitude, those bonded, and those unhappy souls."

The freed slave, therefore, in 1865, could not have known, that his freedom… was only an illusion.

From Howard Zinn, A People's History of the United States:

…Violence began almost immediately with the end of the war. In Memphis, Tennessee, in May of 1866, whites on a rampage of murder killed forty-six Negroes, most of them veterans of the Union army, as well as two white sympathizers. Five Negro women were raped. Ninety homes, twelve schools, and four churches were burned. In New Orleans, in the summer of 1866, another riot against blacks killed thirty-five Negroes and three whites. Mrs. Sarah Song testified before a congressional investigating committee

that had been formed to look into the rash of violent attacks against the newly freed slave:

"Have you been a slave?"

"I have been a slave."

"What did you see of the rioting?"

"I saw them kill my husband; it was on Tuesday night, between ten and eleven o'clock; he was shot in the head while he was in bed sick. There were between twenty and thirty men. They came into the room... Then one stepped back and shot him... he was not a yard from him; he put the pistol to his head and shot him three times. Then one of them kicked him, and another shot him again when he was down. He never spoke after he fell. They then went running right off and did not come back again."

The violence mounted through the late 1860s and early 1870s as the Ku Klux Klan organized raids, lynchings, beatings, burnings... The old white rulers were taking back political power in Mississippi, and everywhere else in the South.

Members of The Grand Old Ku Klux Klan—Ol Massa's Fascist, terrorist enforcers—Armed Guardians of the Old Elite Order—had received their marching orders: From their rich, landowning masters...

It was the boredom of small-town life that led six young Confederate veterans to gather around a fireplace one December evening in 1865 and form a social club. The place was Pulaski, Tennessee, near the Alabama border. When they reassembled a week later, the six young men were full of ideas for their new society. It would be secret, to heighten the amusement of the thing, and the titles for the various officers were to have names as preposterous-sounding as possible, partly for the fun of it and partly to avoid any military or political implications.

Thus, the head of the group was called the Grand Cyclops. His assistant was the Grand Magi; there was to be a Grand Turk to greet all candidates for admission, a Grand Scribe to act as secretary, Night Hawks for messengers and a Lictor to be the guard. The members, when the six young men found some to join, would be called Ghouls. But what name to call the society itself? The founders were determined to come up with something unusual and mysterious. Being well-educated, they turned to Greek. After tossing around a number of ideas, Richard R. Reed suggested the word "kuklos," from which the English words "circle" and "cycle" are derived. Another member, Captain John B. Kennedy, had an ear for alliteration and added the word "clam." After tinkering with the sound for a while, group settled on the "Ku Klux Klan." The selection of the name, chance though it was, had a great deal to do with the Klan's early success. Something about the sound aroused curiosity and gave the fledgling club an immediate air of mystery, as did the initials K.K.K., which were soon to take on such terrifying significance.

Soon after the founders named the Klan, they decided to a bit of showing off and so disguised themselves in sheets and galloped their horses through the quiet streets of little Pulaski. Their ride created such a stir that the men decided to adopt the sheets as the official regalia of the Ku Klux Klan, and they added to the effect by making grotesque masks and tall pointed hats. The founders also performed elaborate initiation ceremonies for new members. Their ceremony was similar to the hazing popular in college fraternities and consisted of blindfolding the candidate, subject him to a series of silly oaths and rough handling, and finally bringing him before a "royal alter" where he was to be invested with "royal crown." The altar turned out to be a mirror and the crown two large donkey's ears. Ridiculous though it sounds today, that was the high point of the earliest activities of the Ku Klux Klan.

—Southern Poverty Law Center, A Hundred Years of Terror.

Astute Ol Massa in his quest to hold his chilluns fastened to the Old Homestead, had come up with a brilliant idea!

Why not take a harmless parlor game and transform that game into a white-sheeted gang of cut-throat marauding murderers, whose only purpose was to restore the Old Order; to keep things, orderly.

And the intended victims of this order rearranging campaign of terror were not just Black malcontents and white Republican carpetbaggers and lowly do-gooders and Negro sympathizers; but any person or thing that stood in the way of its sponsor's ability to keep the Negro on a new kind of plantation; where he could be kept like beasts in the cotton and rice fields: and where he would forever remain—and would forever continue to be the source of free, or cheap labor, that he was intended to be; since Colonial times.

And now in the early days of Reconstruction, Old Massa's (sometimes bloody and violent) message to his former slaves was becoming crystal clear:

The South (America to be exact) was the exclusive domain of the white man, and now, the white man, the rightful heirs of the Constitution, the We in the Big C, the We in, We The People, was now taking the country back from the ones who had been brought here as peons to toil for their masters.

"... White Southerners from all classes of society joined the Klan's ranks. In the name of preserving law and order Klansmen punished newly freed blacks for a variety of reasons, including behaving in an 'impudent' manner toward whites. They whipped the teachers of freedmen's schools and burnt their schoolhouses. But first and foremost, the Klan sought to do away with Republican influence in the South by terrorizing and murdering its party leaders and all those who voted for it."

—PBS, Grant, Reconstruction and the KKK.

The Freedman's Bureau, headed by Union Army General Oliver O. Howard, began operating in 1865.

Its primary function had been to help locate lost families, to teach the newly freed Black man to read, and write, and agents also served as legal advocates for former bondsmen in disputes with the law. The Bureau had also tried to build a bridge between Black and whites that would see them working together as employees and employers, but less than ten years later, nearly all of the gains the Agency had won had been wiped out. In the 1870s with the withdrawal of Union Troops the Klan had moved in and had burned scores of Black schools, and had beaten or killed dozens of teachers.

Tucker Smith, an old-time slave who lived through those dark, turbulent Reconstruction times, interviewed by WPA workers in the 1930s, said:

"… We could not make a move for several years after the war because the KKK were right on our heels and believe me child, we sure did have to step careful… the KKK was on us right now… They did not wait and give us time to adjust ourself to freedom after the war. In fact we were worse off than if we had remained under slavery, as there was countless numbers of our color that were hung, whipped and beat unmerciful through the KKK and the patterrollers together, before we could get readjusted to our new station in life… We have done gone through hell to gain freedom, and a new station in life, for our color and race of people."

But why…? Why was that lingering chill in the air even colder in the 1870s and 1880 than it had been during slavery?

Ol' Massa (the white ruling class) had never been as violent or as savage in his hatred of the Black man, as he was at this moment. Is it about race—and race alone?

"Yes," says Horace Mann Bond in his study of the Alabama Reconstruction, "Racism was an issue, but the accumulations of capital, and the men who controlled them, were as unaffected by attitudinal prejudices as it is possible to be. Without sentiment, without emotion, those who sought profit from an exploitation of... natural resources, turned other men's prejudices and attitudes to their own account, and did so with skill and a ruthless acumen."

Bond goes on to say that in the year 1886, Henry Grady, an editor of the Atlanta Constitution, had spoken at a dinner in New York. In the audience were J. P. Morgan, H. M. Flagler (an associate of Rockefeller), Russell Sage, and Charles Tiffany. His talk was called "The New South" and his theme was: Let bygones be bygones; let us have a new era of peace and prosperity; the Negro was a prosperous laboring class; he had the fullest protection of the laws and the friendship of the southern people. Grady joked about the northerners who had sold slaves to the South, and said the South could now handle its own race problem. He received a rising ovation, and the band played "Dixie."

Now it becomes obvious: The National mood backed up by a distinctly Southern orchestra was playing Dixie; and that meant that that chill in the air was drifting from a distinctly southerly direction.

That *coldness* in the air, the former slave experienced soon after slavery was there because the Southern, and Northern Elites, letting bygones be bygones, had decided that the slave, who was now free, would continue to be what he had been brought to the shores of America to be.

"... Whooosh! That sure was a powerful wicked place, folks gittin' killed and black folks didn't have no protection. They was safer in slave times..."

—Hanna Scott, former slave, interviewed in the 1930s by the WPA.

In the 1870s and 1880s, roads leading in and out of Southern towns and villages were heavily patrolled by night-roving KKK members: who were sometimes spotted galloping side by side with galloping law-enforcing officials.

The Negro had been defined in the Constitution as being the property of the Ruling Class, and now, the Ruling Class was reclaiming its property. The message was in stone: The Negro free or not would remain in captivity.

The message was as stone clear then as it is now: We—whites—are the only owners of this country, and when push comes to shove, We—whites—stand ready, rabid willing, and damned able, to take it back from *any* and *all* non-white undesirables. And in later years, even if it meant colluding with a foreign enemy.

Chapter Two
Jim Crowed on the New Plantation

In the latter part of the nineteenth century the newly freed slaves, sticking to the backwoods and avoiding their former masters as much as possible, would have begun to see strange, puzzling signs cropping up wherever they traveled. Cold, Order-Restoring *signs*—the infamous, **Black Codes**:

The marriage of a white person with a Negro or mulatto or person who shall have one-eighth or more of Negro blood, shall be unlawful and void.

Any negro man and white woman, or any white man and Negro woman, who are not married to each other, who habitually live in and occupy in the nighttime the same room, shall each be punished by imprisonment not exceeding 12 months, or by fine not exceeding five hundred dollars.

The prison warden shall see that the white convicts shall have separate apartments for both eating and sleeping from the Negro convicts.

Separate schools shall be maintained for the children of the white and colored races.

The children of white and colored races committed to reform schools shall be kept entirely separate from each other.

School textbooks shall not be interchangeable between the white and colored schools, but shall continue to be by the race first using them.

It shall be unlawful to conduct a restaurant or other place for the serving of food in the city, at which white and colored people are served in the same room, unless such white and colored persons are effectually separated by a solid partition extending from the floor upward to a distance of seven feet or higher, and unless a separate entrance from the street is provided.

It shall be unlawful for a Negro and white person to play together or in company with each other at any game of pool or billiards.

It shall be unlawful for any amateur white baseball team to play on any vacant lot or baseball diamond within two blocks of a playground devoted to the Negro race, and it shall be unlawful for any amateur-colored baseball tea to play baseball within two blocks of any playground devoted to the white race.

Any person guilty of printing, publishing or circulating matter urging or presenting arguments in favor of social equality or of intermarriage between whites and negroes, shall be guilty of a misdemeanor.

No person or corporation shall require any white female nurse to nurse in wards or rooms in hospitals, either public or private, in which Negro men are placed.

Any person who rents any part of any such building to a Negro person or a Negro family when such building is already in whole or in part in occupancy by a white person or white family shall be guilty of a misdemeanor.

All persons licensed to conduct a restaurant, shall serve either white people exclusively or colored people exclusively and shall not sell to the two races within the same room or under the same license.

Maintain a separate building, on separate grounds, for the admission, care, instruction, and support of all blind persons of the colored or black race.

All persons licensed to conduct the business of selling beer or wine... shall serve either white people exclusively or colored people

exclusively and shall not sell to the two races within the same room at any time.

All circuses, shows, and tent exhibitions, to which the attendance of more than one race is invited, shall provide not less than two ticket offices and not less than two entrances.

Any public hall, theatre, opera house, motion picture show or place of public entertainment which is attended by both white and colored persons shall separate the white race and the colored race.

Any person guilty of printing, publishing or circulating matter urging or presenting arguments in favor of social equality or of intermarriage between whites and Negroes, shall be guilty of a misdemeanor.

The Black Codes, in other words, meant that the former slave for all intents and purposes had been corralled by his former masters and mistresses, and assigned to a new permanent state of servitude.

And he was being told to go on with his life, in purgatory, as if nothing had happened that he should concern himself about—The Old Order was telling the misguided former Bondsman that the Old Order was on the job as it had always been, to protect him, from himself.

Hindering the slave's departure from the plantation even more was the fact that there were still large numbers of plantation owners who, long after the Civil War had simply refused to give up what they considered, and what the Constitution considered, their property.

"…He [master] didn't let us free. We wore chains all the time. When we work, we drug them chains with us. At night he lock us to a tree to keep us from runnin' off… If a slave die, massa made the rest of us tie a rope round he feet and drug him off. Never buried one, it was too much trouble. Massa always say he be rich after the war. He stealin' all the time. He have a whole mountain side where he keep his stock. It was 'bout three years after the war they hung him. Missy turned us a-loose. I had a hard time then. All I had to

**eat was what I could find and steal. I was afraid of everybody. I just
went wild and to the woods."**

—Ben Simpson, former slave, interviewed in the 1930s by the
WPA.

Unbeknownst to the uneducated former bondsman, the Ruling Class
had very secretly been working behind the scenes to reassign its
property to its *new* living quarters. Which, eerily enough, looked very
much like its properties' *old* living quarters.

And forced Negro labor was now in great demand.

Douglas Blackmon, a Wall Street Journal staff reporter, in his article
Alabama's Past, Capitalism and Racism in a Cruel Partnership,
describes how the system was started, and how it worked:

**…The old powers moved quickly to impose a system resembling
the antebellum system in every way except restoration of the
institution of slavery.**

**In Alabama, the local and state authorities collaborated with the
business and corporate powers to impose a system of forced labor,
slavery "in all but name…" The Alabama criminal-judicial system
became a veritable press gang for forcing able-bodied African-
American males into private sector servitude. Arrested and
convicted on trivial and trumped-up charges, they were assigned to
work under brutal, inhuman conditions. The biggest user of forced
labor in Alabama was the Tennessee Coal, Iron and Railroad
Company, a division of the U.S. Steel Corporation. Minor offenses
like vagrancy, foul language, gambling, having sex with whites—all
part of the post-Civil War "Black codes"—would serve as a cover
for police and sheriffs to round up African Americans.**

**This updated form of slavery had been thrust upon the former
bondsman by an all-powerful ruling class that viewed the bondman
simply in terms of dollars and cents.**

As the 1880s and 1890s gave way to the not so new twentieth century, America was now in a rousing celebratory mood.

And this New but not so *new* twentieth century was heralded with fireworks, and band-led parades; nationwide.

Cheap labor was still the roaring engine that was fueling the nation's rapidly growing economy, and the Negro, Atlas-like, was the backbone holding up an entire system of capitalism. And as he was meant to be, he was still the personification, the very embodiment, of cheap, exploitable mule-like labor.

The old Plantation Negro was back!

And his wealth in a country that had turned its back on his wretchedness was now as anemic as it had always been.

His prospects for a prosperous future were now as bleak as it had always been.

And his hope of staying one step ahead of a rope… was now as hopeless, as it had always been.

But in the minds of WE THE PEOPLE, the *only* people, that really mattered, America was *back* as never before: benefitting from a government built on the backs of former slaves, America was once again on top of the world—and was back, where God deemed *it* belonged.

The Black man was once again the ward of his old captors, and *he* was back! Where *he* belonged.

But there were certain segments of the Black population, who protested, sometimes vehemently, and were not willing to go as gently into that good night—without a fight—as those in power had hoped.

W. E. B. Dubois, the head of the newly formed NAACP, was a fierce outspoken voice that not only denounced the white power structure, but was a loud outspoken voice that denounced Black leaders like Booker T. Washington, who advocated a more cautious, go-along-to-get-along, pacifist, philosophy.

Washington believed that Blacks should be patient, accommodating, and willing to perform menial jobs, to achieve economic, and racial equality.

"Our greatest danger is that in the great leap from slavery to freedom we may overlook the fact that the masses of us live by the productions of our hands, and fail to keep in mind that we shall. Prosper in proportion as we learn to dignify and glorify in common labor. It is at the bottom of life we must begin, and not at the top."

Dubois, on the other hand, advanced the theory that Blacks should be college-educated and that college educated Black should be called upon to work in Black communities to uplift those unfortunate souls who had been left behind.

"I believed in the higher education of a Talented Tenth who through their knowledge of modern culture could guide the American Negro into a higher civilization. I know that without this the Negro would have to accept white leadership, and that such leadership would not always be trusted to guide this group into self-realization to its highest cultural possibilities."

He believed that Blacks should agitate for the abolishment of segregation and for the elimination of the social, economic and political barriers that had relegated the Black race into a perpetual system of second-class citizenship.

"I maintain that political power is the beginning of all permanent reform and the only hope for maintaining gains. No permanent improvement in the economic and social condition of Negroes is going to be made so long as they are deprived of political power to support and defend it."

But Washington strenuously objected:

"I believe the Negro, in gaining his equal rights, should be patient and prove himself. In all things purely social we can be as separate as the fingers, yet as the hand in all things essential to mutual progress. The wisest among my race understand that the agitation of questions of social equality is the extremest folly, and that progress in the enjoyment of all the privileges that will come to us must be the result of constant struggle rather than artificial forcing."

But as the debate raged, as to whether Blacks should take a pacifist or a more aggressive radicalized approach to the advancement of the Black race, one thing was perfectly clear:

Re-subjugating an entire race, even a race supposedly as docile as the Black race, had not been *easy*.

It had required the blessings of the white majority, the encouragement of the white states, the dismantlement of the white Constitution, and the heartfelt condolences of the white, very rich, and very powerful men, who pulled the strings behind the scenes.

And as America entered the seventeenth year of that prosperous new twentieth century, all—so far—was well.

But from distant shores, the muffled grumbling sounds of war were in the air. A big war was brewing overseas.

And there was horrific talk in political circles that the Black man was being enlisted to go and fight in that war. *Overseas.*

And that meant that the Black soldier… on foreign soil… could be exposed to some… unhealthy… *ideas?*

Black people [now] contested the boundaries of American democracy, demanded their rights as American citizens, and asserted their very humanity in ways both subtle and dramatic.
—African Americans and World War I, Chad Williams.

And so: as Black men marched off to fight in Europe, here in America, the Black men who stayed behind were sometimes attacked by white mobs for the least provocation.

And on the war-front; as Black warriors fought heroically on the battle-fields, their white company commanders with orders from Washington, sternly suggested that the best favor that foreign mayors and town leaders could do for the Black soldier was to keep him separated from whites. White women, especially. Integrating the two could be bad, very bad, all around, *bad*, for everyone concerned.

The hidden message behind these non-too subtle little warnings to foreign countries was that the Black man must not be accorded the same privileges the white man enjoyed. Not over there. Not over here. Not anywhere. Ever.

But some black soldiers returning home to the South ignored the old ways and refused to bow to the region's century's old *racial codes.*

A veteran in Pine Bluff, Arkansas, refused to get off the sidewalk when told to do so by a white woman. Also, blacks were [now] more likely to meet violence, with violence

> —African Americans and Civil Rights, Michael L. Levine.

The white ruling class looked on these strange developments with increasing alarm.

Were *these* the first rumblings of a racial uprising?

Throughout the South returning black soldiers were assaulted and sometimes forced to run for their lives. And making matters worse, there were full-blown riots in Charleston, South Carolina, Knoxville Tennessee, New York City and Longview, Texas.

In Chicago, beaches throughout Lake Michigan had been segregated. But when a Black man swam accidentally into an area that had been designated for whites only, whites on the beach immediately began throwing rocks; the man drowned. The police were called; but when they refused to arrest members of the mob, outraged Blacks attacked the whites. Whites throughout the city retaliated. Black riders were yanked from streetcars and Black workers in a stockyard were attacked indiscriminately. Black mobs formed and attacked the white mobs, and a full-scale race riot, exploded.

When Black mobs attacked white neighborhoods, order was quickly restored. But as white mobs attacked Black neighborhoods white cops often stood by and refused to intervene; and sometimes joined the white mobs.

The rioting in neighborhoods soon spread throughout the entire city, and lootings, and sporadic gunfire continued for the next three days.

With white America up in arms about the sudden rise in Black-on-white violence sweeping the nation, the 1920s saw the Ku Klux Klan's most prosperous era since the end of the Civil War.

In many parts of the country the Klan dominated local and state politics, with an iron fist. With backing from the Klan politicians in Maine, Oregon, Colorado and Indiana were swept into office in numbers enough to control all levels of government.

And the creeping shadow of The Invisible Empire, was now, stretched clear across the U.S. map.

But as headline grabbing internal conflicts slowly began to decimate the Klan's reputation it slowly began to slink back into dark obscurity.

And suddenly, for the first time in a *long* time, the Black race found itself without an official, government-appointed overseer.

But that… was *all* about to change:

In the 1930s, the Harlem Renaissance was in full swing.

And the Negro who thought of himself as a Black man was now reading and listening to the likes of Langston Hughes, Countee Cullen, Zora Neale Hurston, Claude McKay, Duke Ellington and Louis Armstrong. And there could be no going back to the Old Order. The Negro had gotten a tiny taste of that broader world that Ol Massa had kept so secretly stashed away; knowing, that if the Black man ever got a whiff of life beyond the farm, he would become not a problem, but a nightmare.

Harry Anslinger, a former Prohibition agent, had waged a one-man Holy War against alcohol in the twenties. But now he turned his sights on a Holy War against hemp: a drug that few Americans even knew about.

"Reefer makes darkies think they're as good as white men!" Anslinger raised the alarm in the newsreel cameras of that era, "It is the most violence-causing drug in the history of mankind! You smoke a joint, and you're likely to kill your *brother!"*

This dire assessment of a harmless drug menace to society had been used to dupe the public before; and would be used to dupe it again in the 1970s by the Reagan Administration in its doomsday denunciation of Crack Cocaine.

But would Anslinger's exclamations, like Reagan's proclamations, later prove to be not a war on drugs, but a war on certain folks, in chains?

In the early 1930s jazz musicians had created a monumental headache for Ol Massa, a society-changing, life-altering headache, that could be very threatening to the old way of doing business.

Jazz' race-transcending influence had reached the ears of an increasing number of whites, and Blacks *and* whites were now sitting elbow to elbow in northern Jazz clubs.

That immutable wall between the races, to Ol Massa's horror, was crumbling. More and more whites were being *exposed* to the Black cultural experience. And such exposure could ultimately encourage support for the Negro, for all the wrong reasons: for uppity, Negro institutions, especially, and inevitably, for uppity Negroes themselves.

Jazz was the opposite of everything Harry Anslinger believed in... To Anslinger, this was musical anarchy and evidence of a recurrence of the primitive impulses that lurk in black people, waiting to emerge. "It sounded," his internal memos said, "like the jungles in the dead of night." The lives of the jazzmen, he said, "reek of filth."

Anslinger looked out over a scene filled with rebels like Charlie Parker, Louis Armstrong and Thelonious Monk, and—as the journalist Larry Sloman recorded—he longed to see them all

behind bars. He wrote to all the agents he had sent to follow them and instructed: "Please prepare all cases in your jurisdiction involving musicians in violation of the marijuana laws. We will have a great national round-up arrest of all such persons on a single day. I will let you know what day." His advice on drug raids to his men was always simple: "Shoot first."

One night, in 1939, Billie Holiday stood on stage in New York City and sang a song that was unlike anything anyone had heard before. 'Strange Fruit' was a musical lament against lynching. It imagined black bodies hanging from trees as a dark fruit native to the South. Here was a black woman, before a mixed audience, grieving for the racist murders in the United States. Immediately after, Billie Holiday received her first threat from the Federal Bureau of Narcotics.

—The Hunting of Billie Holiday, Johann Hari.

For her sins, Billie Holiday was hounded into an early grave. Louis Armstrong, Dizzy Gillespie and other well-known musicians received their midnight knocks on the door as well. But something was *missing* in Anslinger's narrative. If drugs were so prevalent among Black musicians, shouldn't there be at least one or two white musicians, somewhere in America, who had innocently, and quite un-willingly, fallen into the depraved camp of the Negro?

One day, Harry Anslinger was told that there were also white women, just as famous as Billie, who had drug problems—but he responded to them rather differently. He called Judy Garland, another heroin addict, in to see him. They had a friendly chat, in which he advised her to take longer vacations between pictures, and he wrote to her studio, assuring them she didn't have a drug problem at all... When he discovered that a Washington society hostess he knew—"a beautiful, gracious lady," he noted—had an illegal drug addiction, he explained he couldn't possibly arrest her because "it would destroy... the unblemished reputation of one of the nation's most honored families." He helped her to wean herself off her addiction slowly, without the law becoming involved. Harry told the public that "the increase [in drug addiction] is practically 100 percent among Negro people," which he stressed was terrifying because already "the Negro population... accounts for 10 percent of the total population, but 60 percent of the addicts."

—The Hunting of Billie Holiday, Johann Hari.

But had Anslinger's crackdown on marijuana, come from higher ups, on the food chain?

"The Drug War is an effort to stimulate fear of dangerous people from who we have to protect ourselves. It is also, a direct form of control of what are called 'dangerous classes', those superfluous people who don't really have a function contributing to profit-making and wealth. They have to be somehow taken care of."

—Noam Chomsky, interviewed by John Veit, High Times.

Mr. Chomsky's assessment provides the rationale, but, was there a motive?

From the nineteenth-century campaigns against opium and alcohol to the crack panic of the 1980s, [War on Drugs] have all been fueled by racism and cultural war, conflated with fear of crime and occasionally abetted by well-intentioned reform impulses... In 1914, Dr. Edward Huntington Williams opined in the New York Times Magazine that "once the Negro has formed the [cocaine] habit, he is irreclaimable. The only method to keep him from taking the drug is by imprisoning him. The movement to prohibit alcohol was part puritanical, part racist..." Liquor will actually make a brute out of a Negro, causing him to commit unnatural crimes, Alabama Rep. Richmond P. Hobson told Congress in 1914, a year after he'd

sponsored the first federal Prohibition bill. He said it had the same effect on white men, but took longer because they were "further evolved."

—Debunking the Hemp Conspiracy Theory,
Steven Wishnia/AlterNet.

Congressmen like Alabama Rep. Richard P. Hobson had enacted Peyote laws giving the police the authority to investigate, prosecute, and imprison Indians, who were now expendable. Like-minded politicians had also enacted Opium laws, that had given the police the authority to investigate, prosecute, and imprison Chinese immigrants who had built the railroads, had also become expendable. And now in the 1930s, like-minded politicians were prepared to enact Marijuana laws, but were they enacted merely to investigate, prosecute, and imprison Blacks? Because they also were now expendable?

If you believe as Noam Chomsky believes, that Drug Wars are a form of control of "dangerous classes," those superfluous people who don't really have a function contributing to profit-making and wealth, then you might be forced to conclude that higher-ups in the food chain, *were indeed* pulling the strings behind the scenes, demonizing the devil weed marijuana—the white woman-attracting, Negro's drug of choice—not just for political reasons, but to enrich corrupt sheriffs, and crooked judges and greedy mining and steel producing companies, that were still very dependent on expendable, *Black*, forced labor.

As the 1940s rolled around, two *new* headaches stood in the wings beckoning for the master's attention, threats, more dangerous, than all the other threats combined, were at the door, knocking.

The first threat came in 1940 with the rumblings of another European war: Black men once again exposed to European ideas would likely be a source of future conflicts when they returned home. The second threat came in October of the same year when political activists A. Philip Randolph and Bayard Rustin called for a March on the Nation's capital, because of discrimination in the defense industry.

President Roosevelt had met with Randolph months earlier. But now the President, not wanting to offend Southern Senators and Congressmen, was refusing to talk or negotiate with Randolph.

But Randolph and Rustin stood firm and would not back down. Instead; they upped the ante by re-naming the march. The 100,000 Member March, a march that would take place in the shadows of Congress and in full view of the American people.

The two activists had called Roosevelt's bluff.

The President was in a quandary. The sight of one hundred thousand Blacks converging on the Nation's capital in the 1940s was a terrifying prospect; the President's popularity and his agenda could both suffer severe setbacks. And how would white America respond? Would Blacks and whites go toe to toe in armed street battles? Would there be rioting in the streets? But more importantly, would there be disruptions to industry, and commerce?

Roosevelt finally acquiesced, signing into law Executive Order 8802: an order declaring that there shall be no discrimination in the employment of workers in the defense industries, or Government, because of race, creed, color, or national origin. The order also called for the establishment of The Fair Employment Practices Commission to investigate complaints of discrimination in wartime.

But there was yet *another* skull-pounding headache lurking in the shadows for the Old Slave Driver, one that would make the long white hairs on his head almost explode: One that would create giant earth-shaking migraines, for him and for his off-springs, for years to come:

In 1942 the Congress of Racial Equality, inspired by the teachings of Mahatma Gandhi, was founded. And four years later CORE would stage the nation's first peaceful sit-in at a whites only restaurant in Chicago: giving birth, and impetus, to the modern-day Civil Rights Movement.

Chapter Three
Plantation Civil Rights

"Black people never had a chance. They never had a plan. They ran from one demonstration and riot to the next. They thought by taking down the signs over the bathrooms and water fountains, or where Blacks could sit, somehow you were dealing with racism. Allowing a Black person to sit on the bus is immaterial. Allowing a Black person to go into a hotel is a waste of time. The question should be: Can he pay to get out of the hotel... It's about economics...! And, we never created an institution that would educate our kids on how to deal with racism, one that would give them a plan so they could be trained as leaders. So from 1966 to 1996, Black youth fell through the crack because we let them down."

—Dr. Claud Johnson, former assistant secretary of Commerce.

As Black America entered the 1950s... that old question of why, emerged, yet again. *Why* did it seem like the harder Black folks worked the farther they remained behind the white man? *What* was going on, here?

Were Blacks just plain genetically lazy?

Were they so intellectually challenged, so unaware of their surroundings, that they couldn't *see* all of the wonderful opportunities that *all* Americans enjoy? Were they just *naturally... inferior...*?

Anyone could plainly see that they only had *themselves*, to blame, so what in the name of Robert E. Lee could possibly be going on here?

But in the early 1950s, the caught-off-guard white ruling class had *no* time to ponder the awful *whys,* and the *wherefores*.

A revolution—smoking, over the horizon—was quietly, but steadily, approaching.

In 1954, the Supreme Court ordered the desegregation of public schools and other public facilities.

And in 1955, fourteen-year-old Emmett Till was horrifically beaten to death in Mississippi, for allegedly whistling at a white woman, and his death, eliciting outrage worldwide, legitimized, and energized, the struggling and sometimes inept Civil Rights Movement.

A short three months later, Rosa Parks would refuse to give up her seat to a white man on a bus, and as horrified America looked on the Montgomery Bus Boycott led by Martin Luther King was underway.

In the 1920s J. Edgar Hoover had worked to sabotage the Marcus Garvey Back to Africa Movement. The idea, no matter how unrealistic, of cheap labor, suddenly vanishing from the economy, had made Garvey a marked man; a Moses-like exodus from the land of the white man could not be allowed to happen. Hoover had thrown the full weight of his newly created crime-busting unit into destroying Garvey. But finding no clear-cut evidence that Garvey was engaged in fraudulent activities Hoover was finally able to convict and deport the mischief-maker out of the country on bogus trumped-up mail fraud charges.

And now, in the 1950s, using many of the same techniques he had used on the insurrectionist Garvey, Hoover created a tactical surveillance unit that would track the behavior of the country's newest most wanted law-breaker in America: And files detailing Martin Luther King's every move… over the course of five years… would balloon to 17,000 pages.

Cointelpro: a government sponsored program that had been designed to increase factionalism, and cause disruptions and win defections inside the Communist party, now had its sights on the Black man, and especially, its leaders.

Hoover had decreed that there were certain elements inside the Civil Rights Movement that had ties to the Communist Party. This was his *stated* excuse for targeting the Movement's leaders. But long after the members of the Civil Rights Movement had been shown to have no connections to Communism, the secret surveillance continued.

Malcolm X's fiery non-compromising speeches had condemned King's strategy of nonviolence as being unrealistic. And his advocacy of violence in the face of violence was very unsettling not only to King, but to the ears of J. Edgar Hoover.

"The only revolution, in which the goal is loving your enemy, is the Negro revolution. Revolution is bloody, revolution is hostile, revolution knows no compromise—revolution overturns and destroys everything that gets in the way."

And like MLK, the speeches of Malcolm X would be singled out, for close, daily scrutiny… by the Agency. And Agency officials would have liked nothing better than to create a strained conflict between the two men. But Malcolm had grown to admire Dr. King, and in his last speech, The Ballot or the Bullet, he spoke as a man, on a fence-mending mission:

…Although I'm still a Muslim, I'm not here tonight to discuss my religion. I'm not here to try and change your religion. I'm not here to argue or discuss anything that we differ about; because it's time for us to submerge our differences and realize that it is best for us to first see that we have the same problem, a common problem, a problem that will make you catch hell whether you're a Baptist, or a Methodist, or a Muslim, or a nationalist. Whether you're educated or illiterate, whether you live on the boulevard or in the alley, you're going to catch hell just like I am. We're all in the same boat and we all are going to catch the same hell from the same man.

Malcolm X, alias Detroit Red, a former small-time hood who had burst upon the world's stage preaching the Black Muslim belief that the white man was the Devil incarnate. But a pilgrimage to Mecca and his extensive travels throughout the Middle East had given him a more mature, less xenophobic outlook on life. And as he began to reach out not just to the militant wing of the Movement but to King's nonviolent wing, he realized that if the Movement was to survive, the various elements of that movement had to coalesce into a united single unit; with no one unit being the Ultimate Decider.

And now, as the mid-1960s loomed on the horizon, the Civil Rights March on Washington was suddenly televised, live—and unedited—and TV sets in living rooms nationwide showed a massive sea of Black faces spread out along the Washington Mall cheering King's, I Have a Dream, speech. And among the millions of viewers who were watching that historic moment, were agents from the F.B.I. And while King's doctrine of nonviolent peaceful protest was winning the hearts of most American's, that same doctrine in the eyes of the FBI, was proof positive, that King had overstepped his bounds.

In late November of 1964, the Civil Rights leader received a mysterious package in the mail. This *mysterious* package was delivered a few days after the massive March on Washington, coincidentally, and not long after J. Edgar Hoover had gone on television calling Martin Luther King the most notorious liar in the country. Hoover had also called King the most *dangerous* Negro in America.

The *package…* contained a letter, and an audio recording. But, the letter, was no ordinary letter; for it called on King to commit suicide.

"King, look into your heart. You know you are a complete fraud and a great liability to all of us Negroes… You are no clergyman and you know it. I repeat you are a colossal fraud and an evil, vicious one at that.

You could have been our greatest leader. You, even at an early age have turned out to be not a leader but a dissolute, abnormal

moral imbecile. We will now have to depend on our older leaders like Wilkins, a man of character and thank God we have others like him. But you are done. Your "honorary" degrees, your Nobel Prize (what a grim farce) and other awards will not save you. King, I repeat you are done.

There is only one thing left for you to do. You know what it is. You have just 34 days in which to do it (this exact number has been selected for a specific reason; it has definite practical significance). You are done. There is but one way out for you. You better take it before your filthy, abnormal fraudulent self is bared to the nation."

In 1951, J. Edgar Hoover had turned to black NAACP director, Roy Wilkins, to spread a vicious smear campaign against noted singer and Civil Rights icon, Paul Robeson. An FBI inspired letter pushed by Wilkins, had portrayed Robeson as a communist sympathizer; and as Robeson traveled across Africa, the letter warned Africans that they should remember that a communist does not speak for the average American Negro.

And now, years later… in this suicide letter… sent to King by the FBI, Wilkins, and other leaders of his ilk, had the kind of character the FBI could admire, "and thank God we have others like him," the letter had stated.

But *who* were those *others*, like Wilkins? That could be *controlled?* And: did those other, *controllable* Negroes, become the future leaders of the Civil Rights Movement after King's assassination?

But King was undeterred.

His home and his hotel rooms had been bugged. He was being threatened by a mysterious letter-writer who had told him that the number 34 was very significant, and that his days were over.

But, as 1965 rolled around, King took his subversive establishment-shaking protest to the streets of Selma Alabama; where he was quickly arrested: for leading two hundred marchers in a protest against unfair voting laws.

As King sat confined in a Selma Alabama jail cell, his arch rival, and fellow revolutionist, Malcolm X, showed up in Selma, and met with King's wife, Coretta. He assured her that he had not come to Selma to make life miserable for her husband. He had come, "because if white people realize what the alternative is, perhaps they will be more willing to hear Dr. King."

Malcolm had made the journey to Selma knowing that his every move was now being watched by the FBI.

"Documents released under the Freedom of Information Act reveal a pattern of surveillance and harassment by the FBI, CIA, and the New York City Police Department's 'red squad'. They show an ongoing fear of Malcolm as an actual and potential leader of a black America independent of the norms of subservience and coercion and, most frighteningly, connected to the storm of movements for change worldwide."

—Monthly Review, John J. Simon.

On February 4, 1965, the day before he had met with Coretta King, two men who identified themselves as FBI agent Beckwith and FBI agent Fulton had met with Malcolm, and in a secretly taped recording, had offered to make a deal with him, as they had offered to make a deal with King.

FBI Agent 1: It's probably what you assume we've come here for. To obtain any information you want to give us about the Muslims.

Malcolm: No, I didn't assume anything—

FBI Agent 1: (laughing nervously) That's a very general statement on my part. But uh, as you know, we follow the activities of the Muslims. As best we can. But we're always looking for other avenues, of information, and who better, than, you know, the head

of the Muslims...? That is, up to a month ago, before your suspension...?

FBI Agent 2: How's your suspension status?

Malcolm: No one knows what Mr. Muhammad does, you'll have to ask him.

FBI Agent 2: You're not working now, teaching now?

Malcolm: Well I'm still under the suspension...

FBI Agent 1: One of the reasons we've picked this particular time, to uh, contact you, is because of this suspension...

Malcolm: The suspension was brought about by my own doing.

FBI Agent 1: Yeah. Exactly. But, uh, who knows what was in your mind... when you did receive the suspension... You know, bitterness could have entered into it... It would not be... illogical, for someone, who had spent so many years doing something, and gets suspended...

Malcolm: No, it should make him stronger, because, it makes him realize that law applies to the enforcer, as well as those who are under the enforcement of the enforcer.

FBI Agent 2: You've taken nearly a perfect attitude, toward the thing, which is almost un-human, really. You've taken the attitude that Mr. Muhammad wants everyone to take a beating, chastisement, which is fine... (laughs)... m-more power to you! But you see from our viewpoint, there's, uh, at least a chance, that someone suspended from your organization, for some reason or another, and we talk to them, and they uh... [(unintelligible static]... I assume you'll uh, resume your duties, we'd uh, as you know, we'd be interested, in having you help us out...?

Malcolm: Help you out to do what? We're always helping out the government... We're at least able to reform the people who have been made criminals in this society. And anyway to help out other than that, I wouldn't even know how to begin.

FBI Agent 1: Well, what we're interested in, uh, basically, are the people who belong, the name of members...

Malcolm: My telephone number is OL1-6320.

FBI Agent 2: Now, by this, by this suggestion—

Malcolm: That's like telling you that the sun shines from the East.

FBI Agent 2: Well, no comment… And, uh, the teachings, the plans, the programs…?

Malcolm: No teachings are more public than ours. And I don't think you'll find anyone more blunt in stating it publicly. As we do. I don't think you can go anywhere on this earth, and find anyone who expresses their views on matters more candidly, than we do.

FBI Agent 2: I can only agree with you. That's right, you're right. The main thing is, uh, there is a certain area of responsibility, that's getting into our angle of it. What we really want is, part of the names, of all of those who belong, who they are, their identification—

Malcolm: I don't even know them.

FBI Agent 2: Uh, you keep no records…?

Malcolm: That's not my job. I'm just a preacher.

FBI Agent 2: Yeah, but somebody up there keeps the records—

Malcolm: I don't know who. I don't have any knowledge of those kinds of things. With all of these other responsibilities that I've had, it would be difficult for me to worry about names. Plus: You would insult my intelligence, asking me for them. In fact you insult your own, because it would mean that your own intelligence isn't heavy enough, to weigh me, and do not know in advance what I'm going to say when you ask that question.

FBI Agent 2: Well, without getting into semantics, uh, you never know till you ask.

Malcolm: There's nothing semantic here, evidently, it goes to your psychology.

FBI Agent 1: We've had people, uh, not this particular group, but other groups—

Malcolm: Oh yes-s.

FBI Agent 1: Who have been just as vociferous against whatever we're investigating, communism, make that a case example. A communist for twenty years, you know. You go and interview them, you don't want to, but you go anyway. Knock on the door. Where have you been? Oh I want to tell you something. You never know the answer. That's happened so many times. Uh… sometimes… uh, your word isn't convincing, but sometimes, uh, money brings out the information…? Don't uh, mean to insult you here…

Malcolm: According to Dillon, what's his name, the Secretary of the Treasury? This government's money is in such trouble—

FBI Agent 1: (laughing) Yeah but you can still spend it!

Malcolm: Still. According to your government economists, the dollar itself is in such trouble, that a person would be a fool to sell his soul for one of these decreasing dollars.

FBI Agent 2: Oh, I… couldn't agree with you more…! You'd be a fool to sell your soul if the dollar is increasing! But this has nothing to do with selling your soul. I mean, if you uh, uh, want to look at it that way, OK, but—

Malcolm: Depends on how you look at it.

FBI Agent 2: Sure.

Malcolm: You insult my intelligence; not only do they insult my intelligence, not only that, they insult me, period, if they think I would tell them anything.

FBI Agent 1: But uh, it-it would uh, it would be [garbled] in many ways, it uh, might be of some benefit to your [new?] organization, you know. If in fact we can eliminate people…

Malcolm: There's no government agency that can ever expect any information out of me. That is in any way detrimental to any religious group, or Black group for that matter, in this country. No government agency; because they should use that same energy to go and find who bombed that church down there in Alabama. If these government agencies spent as much money, and time, and energy—

FBI Agent 1: You know what somebody in the South is saying today? That, if you people would go up north and investigate the Muslims, with the same energy you're trying to find this bombing character—

Malcolm: But Muslims don't bomb churches. If we broke the laws… they'd have us in jail tomorrow.

—The FBI Tries to Bribe Malcolm X, secretly recorded audio.

African Diaspora News.

Did other Black leaders in the 1960s receive a knock on the door from the FBI—from pleasant talking men with friendly attitudes?

The aim of J. Edgar Hoover's CointelPro operation had been to subvert, *convert*, or, if necessary, *eliminate*, any and all threats, to national security. And that meant that Malcolm and Martin now had bright red targets on their backs making them Public Enemies Number One, and Number Two. Enemies, of the State.

On February 5, 1965, Malcolm flew to Britain where he was to address the Council of African Organizations in London. On February 6, he set out for France. But France denied him the right to enter its territory. On February 14, back in America his next stop was Detroit Michigan, where he would deliver his *last* speech; before a large enthusiastic crowd assembled at the old Ford Auditorium.

Distinguished guests, brothers and sisters, ladies and gentlemen, friends and enemies… I was in a house last night that was bombed; my own. It didn't destroy all my clothes, not all, but you know what happens when fire dashes through—they get smoky. The only thing I could get my hands on before leaving was what I have on now.

It isn't something that made me lose confidence in what I am doing, because my wife understands and I have children from this size on down, and even in their young age they understand. I think they would rather have a father or brother or whatever the situation may be who will take a stand in the face of any kind of reaction from

narrow-minded people rather than to compromise and later on have to grow up in shame and in disgrace.

So I just ask you to excuse my appearance. I don't normally come out in front of people without a shirt and a tie...

I might point out right here... [that there] are four different types of people in the Western Hemisphere... all of whom have Africa as a common heritage... Colonialism or imperialism, as the slave system of the West is called, is not something that's just confined to England or France or the United States. But the interests in this country are in cahoots with the interests in France and the interests in Britain. It's one huge complex or combine, and it creates what's known as not the American power structure or the French power structure, but it's an international power structure. And this international power structure is used to suppress the masses of dark-skinned people all over the world and exploit them of their natural resources.

[And] since the French government and the British government and this government here, the United States, know that I have been almost fanatically stressing the importance of the Afro-American uniting with the African and working as a coalition, especially in areas which are of mutual benefit to all of us. And the governments in these different places were frightened because they know that the Black revolution [is] taking place on the outside of their house.

The newly awakened people all over the world pose a problem for what's known as Western interests, which is imperialism, colonialism, racism, and all these other negative isms or vulturistic isms...

One of the shrewd ways that they use the press... is that they feed these statistics to the public, primarily the white public. Because... whatever the government is going to do, it always wants the public on its side, whether it's the local government, state government, [or] federal government. So they use the press to create images... showing the high crime rate in the Negro community. As soon as this high crime rate is emphasized through the press, then people begin to look upon the Negro community as a community of criminals.

And then any Negro in the community can be stopped in the street. "Put your hands up," and they pat you down. You might be a doctor, a lawyer, a preacher, or some other kind of Uncle Tom. But despite your professional standing, you'll find that you're the same victim as the man who's in the alley. Just because you're Black and you live in a Black community, which has been projected as a community of criminals. This is done. And once the public accepts this image also, it paves the way for a police-state type of activity in the Negro community. They can use any kind of brutal methods to suppress Blacks because "they're criminals anyway." And what has given this image? The press again, by letting the power structure or the racist element in the power structure use them in that way.

A very good example was the riots that took place here during the summer: If you'll notice, they referred to the rioters as vandals, hoodlums, thieves. They skillfully took the burden off the society for its failure to correct these negative conditions in the Black community. It took the burden completely off the society and put it right on the community by using the press to make it appear that the looting and all of this was proof that the whole act was nothing but vandals and robbers and thieves, who weren't really interested in anything other than that which was negative. And I hear many old, dumb, brainwashed Negroes who parrot the same old party line that the man handed down in his paper.

It was not the case that they were just knocking out store windows ignorantly. In Harlem, for instance, all of the stores are owned by white people, all of the buildings are owned by white people. Black people are just there, paying rent, buying the groceries. But they don't own the stores... [They] don't even own the homes that they live in. This is all owned by outsiders... It costs us more money to live in the slum, than it costs them to live down on Park Avenue. Black people in Harlem know this. And the white merchants charge us more money for food in Harlem—and it's the cheap food, it's the worst food; and we have to pay more money for it than the man has to pay for it downtown. So Black people know that they're being exploited and that their blood is being sucked and they see no way out of it... This is what makes them knock down the store windows and set fire to things...

When you begin to start thinking for yourself, you frighten them, and they try and block you getting to the public, for fear that if the public listens to you, then the public won't listen to them anymore. And they've got certain Negroes whom they have to keep blowing up in the papers to make them look like leaders. So that the people will keep on following them, no matter how many knocks they get on their heads following him. This is how the man does it, and if you don't wake up and find out how he does it, I tell you, they'll be building gas chambers and gas ovens pretty soon—I don't mean those kind you've got at home in your kitchen.

First they fanned the flame in such a manner to create hysteria in the mind of the public. And then they shift gears and fan the flame in a manner designed to get the sympathy of the public. And once they go from hysteria to sympathy, their next step is to get the public to support them in whatever act they're getting ready to go down with. You're dealing with a cold calculating international machine, that's so criminal in its objectives and motives that it has the seeds of its own destruction, right within... In your struggle it's like standing on a revolving wheel: you're running, but you're not going anywhere. You run faster and faster and the wheel just goes faster and faster. You don't ever leave the spot that you're standing in...

1965 will be the longest and hottest and bloodiest year of them all. It has to be, not because you want it to be, or I want it to be, or we want it to be, but because the conditions that created these explosions in 1963 are still here; the conditions that created explosions in '64 are still here. You can't say that you're not going to have an explosion and you leave the condition, the ingredients, still here. As long as those ingredients, explosive ingredients, remain, then you're going to have the potential for explosion on your hands.

And it is for this reason that it is so important for you and me to start organizing among ourselves, intelligently, and try to find out: What are we going to do…?

Don't let the power structure maneuver you into a time wasting battle with others when you could be involved in something that's constructive and getting a real job done.

And one of our first programs is to take our problem out of the civil rights context and place it at the international level, of human rights, so that the entire world can have a voice in our struggle. If we keep it at civil rights, then the only place we can turn for allies is within the domestic confines of America. But when you make it a human rights struggle, it becomes international, and then you can open the door for all types of advice and support from our brothers in Africa, Latin America, Asia, and elsewhere. So it's very, very important. That's our international aim, that's our external aim.

I say again that I'm not a racist. I don't believe in any form of segregation or anything like that. I'm for the brotherhood of everybody, but I don't believe in forcing brotherhood upon people who don't want it. Long as we practice brotherhood among ourselves, and then others who want to practice brotherhood with us, we practice it with them also, we're for that. But I don't think that we should run around trying to love somebody who doesn't love us.

Thank you.

And then, eight days later, on February 22, 1965, New Yorkers woke up to find the following article in the New York Post:

They came early to the Audubon Ballroom, perhaps drawn by the expectation that Malcolm X would name the men who firebombed his home last Sunday, streaming from the bright afternoon sunlight into the darkness of the hall...

Then a man was on the stage, saying:

"... I now give you Brother Malcolm. I hope you will listen, hear, and understand..."

When, after more than a minute the crowd quieted, Malcolm looked up and said, "A salaam aleikum (Peace be unto you)" and the audience replied "Wa aleikum salaam (And unto you, peace)."

Bespectacled and dapper in a dark suit, his sandy hair glinting in the light, Malcolm said: "Brothers and sisters." He was interrupted by two men in the center of the ballroom, about four rows in front and to the right of me, who rose and, arguing with each other, moved forward. Then there was a scuffle in the back of the room and, as I turned my head to see what was happening, I heard Malcolm X say his last words: "Now, now brothers, break it up," he said softly. "Be cool, be calm."

Then all hell broke loose. There was a muffled sound of shots and Malcolm, blood on his face and chest, fell limply back over the chairs behind him. The two men who had approached him ran to the exit on my side of the room shooting wildly behind them as they ran.

I fell to the floor, got up, tried to find a way out of the bedlam.

Malcolm's wife, Betty, was near the stage, screaming in a frenzy. "They're killing my husband," she cried. "They're killing my husband..."

At an exit I saw some of Malcolm's men beating with all their strength on two men. Police were trying to fight their way toward the two. The press of the crowd forced me back inside.

I saw a half-dozen of Malcolm's followers bending over his inert body on the stage, their clothes stained with their leader's blood. Then they put him on a litter while guards kept everyone off the

platform. A woman bending over him said: "He's still alive. His heart's beating…"

I spotted a phone booth in the rear of the hall, fumbled for a dime, and called a photographer. Then I sat there, the surprise wearing off a bit, and tried desperately to remember what had happened. One of my first thoughts was that this was the first day of National Brotherhood Week 3.

—Thomas Skinner, "I saw Malcolm Die," The New York Post, February 22, 1965.

Documents later released by the FBI show that J. Edgar Hoover had told the agency's New York office to "do something about Malcolm X."

Hoover had hoped to prevent the rise of a Black Messiah, who could unify, and electrify the Black Race.

And that messiah, in the eyes of the Bureau, was The One, whom they had tried to bribe; with an iron-clad promise to eliminate the competition.

But Martin Luther King seemed as stunned by Malcomb's assassination as the rest of the nation, as he stood before network television cameras.

"Nothing can be accomplished through violence. It only leads to new and more complex social problems… It is unhealthy for our nation."

But King's statement, that nothing can be accomplished, through violence, fell on deaf ears. Malcolm's dire prediction… that 1965 would be the deadliest year in the history of the Civil Rights Movement… would soon be put to the test.

Less than a month later, on March 7, 1965, Civil Rights activists John Lewis and Hosea Williams, led a march from Selma Alabama towards Montgomery Alabama; but as they reached the Edmund Pettis Bridge; they were met by state troopers, where some protestors were severely beaten with clubs; while others were tear gassed, or sprayed with high-pressure water hoses.

The protestors were swept back in a fog of tear gas.

But two weeks later, on March 21, more than three thousand protestors again gathered at the Edmund Pettis Bridge; and this time, with the entire nation watching the event on television, the marchers began their slow, uncertain march across the bridge, towards Montgomery Alabama. And this time, they met *no* interference from local *or* state officials.

The following year on October 15, 1966, Bobby Seale, and Huey Newton, heeding the advice of Malcolm X, formed The Black Panther Party. In February of 1967 Eldridge Cleaver—who in later years would become an upright right-wing Republican extremist—lent his hand to the struggle. Cleaver would later change the organization's original slogan, Power to the People, to Black Power, infusing in its doctrine a noticeably Marxist, anti-American sentiment—a sentiment, that was almost guaranteed to alienate not only white America, but J. Edgar Hoover as well.

Soon afterwards, whipping the flames of hysteria, Hoover announced to the world that The Black Panther Party was the "single greatest threat to the internal security of the United States."

And suddenly Hoover had set his eagle-eyes on the newest... single... greatest... threats to the internal security of the United States, and, as he had done in the days of John Dillinger, Machine Gun Kelly, Baby-Face Nelson, and the notorious Billie Holliday, he rolled up his sleeves and reported to work *protecting* America.

Hoover's FBI had a "counter-intelligence" program (COINTELPRO) which combated whatever group Hoover declared as dangerous. The aim of the program, in Hoover's words, was "to neutralize their leaders, their spokesmen, membership and supporters." The program included infiltrating the organization, and stirring up differences within the Panther Party.

Harassment of the Panthers was at a peak in 1968 and 1969. Local police watched the Panthers closely and made numerous arrests on whatever charges they imagined might be plausible— arrests that could not be sustained by the courts. Panthers were harassed with high bail and with heavy fees in retrieving their cars from police impoundment...

"There were shootouts between the police and the Panthers. The police killed twenty Panthers, including a Chicago Panther that law enforcement saw as especially dangerous: Fred Hampton. Hampton was a good orator and a capable organizer... He was having success in Chicago drawing people to the Panthers. Then the police raided his headquarters at around four in the morning, entering the building in a blaze of gunfire, killing the guard who was asleep with his shotgun just behind the front door, and firing a volley of rounds into the bedroom where Hampton was known to be. Hampton was severely wounded but still alive. He died when a couple of more rounds were fired into his head."

—The Sixties and the Seventies from Berkeley to Woodstock, Microhistory.com.

In 1968, Hoover's Cointelpro operatives had infiltrated and was beginning to separate, and decimate, the Panthers, from the inside out.

Meanwhile, on February 4 of the same year, the FBI also had Martin Luther King under intense observation, when he stood before a packed congregation that had gathered at his home church (Ebenezer Baptist), to hear his famous Drum Major Speech.

"God didn't call America to do what she's doing in the world now. God didn't call America to engage in a senseless, unjust war as the war in Vietnam. And we are criminals in that war. We've committed more war crimes almost than any nation in the world, and I'm going to continue to say it. And we won't stop it, because of our pride, and our arrogance as a nation."

King's activities and his speeches seemed to give credence to Hoover's claim that King was merely a fraudulent anti-American agitator. Certain, now, that the Civil Rights leader was under the control of Communist advisors, Bureau agents, with Hoover's blessings, intensified their covert activities, placing King into a veritable fish bowl: where he was watched, and monitored, 24 hours a day.

But King outwardly seemed undaunted. He had a busy schedule. An upcoming Poor People's March was on the drawing board, and, as a last-minute change in his itinerary… there was a garbage strike, in Memphis Tennessee… to consider.

Black Sanitation workers in Memphis had had enough; they wanted higher wages, better working conditions, and less whip. Receiving none of the above, they simply walked off the plantation and took to the streets.

King had planned a trip to Africa; but the unrest in Memphis was making headlines. King changed his itinerary.

And on March 29, the white ruling elites in Memphis were dislodged from a permanent state of apathy by the images on their television sets, that showed more than five thousand noisy, black-faced sign-waving protestors swarming the downtown streets; bringing traffic, and commerce, to a worrisome stand-still. A sea of angry Black and white faces had joined hands in a common cause: and *that* was even more worrisome. And their grating, irritating, chants of, "I am a man! I am a man! I am a man!" was not only revolting, and anti-business, but it also had that distinct tone and tenor of something… too terrible to talk about.

But the protest quickly veered out of control. Unruly thugs had swirled from nearby neighborhoods, screaming, and hurtling rocks into several downtown storefront windows. Looting, violence, and bedlam erupted, and in the chaos, a sixteen-year-old Black boy was killed by Memphis police officers. Four thousand national guardsmen were quickly dispatched to the scene; and a city-wide curfew was clamped down hard on the city. King had been forced to call off the protest; but he vowed to return in the very near future.

On April 3, 1968, two months after the beginning of the strike, King came back to Memphis. And it was on this date that he gave his famous, Mountain Top speech.

"Thank you very kindly, my friends... I'm delighted to see each of you here tonight in spite of a storm warning... Something is happening in Memphis; something is happening in our world... I can remember when Negroes were just going around scratching where they didn't itch, and laughing when they were not tickled. But that day is all over. We mean business now, and we are determined to gain our rightful place in God's world.

We've got to stay together and maintain unity. You know, whenever Pharaoh wanted to prolong the period of slavery in Egypt, he had a favorite, favorite formula for doing it. What was that? He kept the slaves fighting among themselves. But whenever the slaves get together, something happens in Pharaoh's court, and he cannot hold the slaves in slavery. When the slaves get together, that's the beginning of getting out of slavery.

...I don't know what will happen now; we've got some difficult days ahead... But I'm not concerned about that now... I'm happy tonight; I'm not worried about anything; and I'm not fearing any man!"

King had said that God had allowed him to go up to the mountaintop, and that he had *seen* the Promised Land, adding, that he may not get *there*, with his supporters, but as a people they would get there together.

On the evening of April 4, 1968, Martin Luther King and his friends were getting dressed to have dinner with Memphis minister Billy Kyles. King was in Room 306 on the second floor and hurried to get dressed since they were, as usual, running a bit late. While putting on his shirt and using Magic Shave Powder to shave, King chatted with Ralph Abernathy about an upcoming event...

Kyles was just a couple steps down the stairs and Abernathy was still inside the motel room when the shot rang out. Some of the men initially thought it a car backfire, but others realized it was a rifle shot. King had fallen to the concrete floor of the balcony with a large, gaping wound covering his right jaw.

Abernathy ran out of his room to see his dear friend fallen, laying in a puddle of blood. He held King's head saying, "Martin, it's all right. Don't worry. This is Ralph. This is Ralph."

Kyles had gone into a motel room to call an ambulance while others encircled King. Marrell McCollough, an undercover Memphis police officer, grabbed a towel and tried to stop the flow of blood. Though King was unresponsive, he was still alive—but only barely.

Within fifteen minutes of the shot, Martin Luther King arrived at St. Joseph's Hospital on a stretcher with an oxygen mask over his face. He had been hit by a .30-06 caliber rifle bullet that had entered his right jaw, then traveled through his neck, severing his spinal cord, and stopped in his shoulder blade.

The doctors tried emergency surgery, but the wound was too serious. Martin Luther King, Jr. was pronounced dead at 7:05 p.m.

—Martin Luther King Jr. Assassinated, Jennifer Rosenberg.

Ten years later: The Church Committee had been formed to look into the assassination of Dr. King, and during the hearings, it became obvious that the FBI had clearly overstepped its bounds in its day-to-day surveillance of the murdered Civil Rights leader.

Senator Mondale: I'm trying to find out what it was, that impelled the FBI, to pursue Martin Luther King with such an obsession. It was not any suspicion of a commission of a federal crime, none of [your] literature showed a single suggestion that Martin Luther King had committed, or was about to commit a crime, is that correct?

White FBI Agent: That's correct.

Black FBI Agent: But sir, at this point, what was being done [by Dr. King] involved challenges to local law officers, and there is the very strong suggestion that King was seen as rallying the lawbreakers and would-be lawbreakers… If we look at what might have gotten the Bureau started, at the same time he was extremely critical of the Bureau's own law enforcement efforts. And we see throughout these documents… that it is taboo to criticize the Bureau and particularly the Director.

Senator Mondale: Was he [Dr. King] ever charged for any violence? Did he ever participate in violence?

Black FBI Agent: No.

Senator Mondale: Was it ever alleged that he was about to participate in violence?

Black FBI Agent: No.

Senator Mondale: So it was neither the fear of a commission of a crime, or the commission of violence, was there ever any serious charge that he himself was a communist?

White FBI Agent: No such charge was ever made.

Senator Mondale: So what was left then was a decision, on the part of some persons, or person, within the FBI, that he should nevertheless be pursued. And the basis for that apparently was political. The decision that he was dangerous, or potentially dangerous, to someone's notion, of what this country should be doing; and a further theory that the FBI possessed the ability to enter into this field, and investigate and to intimidate, and seek to neutralize and replace a Civil Rights leader that they thought to be politically unacceptable. Is that correct?

White FBI Agent: Yes.

Senator Mondale: And the tactics they used, apparently, had no end. Micro phonic surveillance of hotel rooms, informants, letters signed by phony names to friends and organizers, it involved even plans to replace him with someone the FBI was to select as a Civil Rights leader, is that correct?

White FBI Agent: Yes, but that plan… didn't get very far—

Senator Mondale: But it was seriously considered. And Mr. Hoover pinned a note to that suggestion, commending its author. Correct?

White FBI Agent [after consulting with lawyer]… Yes…

Senator Mondale: There was also a request to the Pope not so see [Dr. King], a request to a major university not to grant him a doctorate degree.

White Agent: …That's correct… After the march on Washington. There was acceleration: he was defined, because of his speech… as the most dangerous, and effective leader in the country, and there was a paper battle within the Bureau as to how best to attack him. And he was attacked. After TIME magazine named him man of the year, again, the Bureau finds that reprehensible, and believes it must attack and destroy: When he was given the Nobel Prize, again they [sought] to discredit Dr. King with the persons who met him back from that award. When he began to speak out against the Vietnam War, there's a new crescendo of efforts by the Bureau to discredit and destroy Dr. King.

Ralph Abernathy (SCLC president, who would testify later): "It is my feeling, that the assassination of Dr. King was part of a conspiracy, and I do believe that some individuals in very high places, of our government, were involved in this conspiracy. And it is the same conspiracy that eliminated and destroyed President Kennedy, Senator [Robert] Kennedy, Malcolm X, Medgar Evers, and so many other freedom and human rights individuals."

But Abernathy was not a lone voice in the wilderness; other cries of foul play were being raised by other noted Civil Rights leaders. Andrew Young, who had been at King's side throughout most of his Civil Rights career, said: "I think the issue is that the neo-Fascist police state mentality, that pervaded the intelligence community, is [still] a danger to America to this day."

In April of 1967 James Earl Ray had escaped from prison by hiding inside of a bakery van. A year later, in April of 1968, documents show that he checked into a boarding house that had a clear bathroom view of the Lorraine Motel.

Shortly after King was murdered, as he stood on the balcony of the Lorraine Motel, a rifle draped in a cloth was dropped at the doorway of a nearby business. Along with the rifle were a number of items that led the police to broadcast an all-points bulletin for James Earl Ray, who—like the assassins of Malcolm X and John Kennedy and later Robert Kennedy—would be identified as a lone gun assassin.

But was James Earl Ray a lone assassin?

In December of 1999 a wrongful death lawsuit was filed by the King family. The lawsuit named a restaurant owner named Lloyd Jowers, and other unknown co-conspirators including agencies of the U.S. Government as plaintiffs; as the ones who had conspired, and carried out the assassination.

Almost 32 years after King's murder… a court extended the circle of responsibility for the assassination beyond the late scapegoat James Earl Ray to the United States Government.

In 1993 Lloyd Jowers told his story to Sam Donaldson on Prime Time Live. He explained how he had been asked to participate in the murder of King, told how a decoy (Ray) was in on the plot, and that the plotters had assured him that the police wouldn't be on duty at the appointed time.

Jowers said the man who asked him to help in the murder was a Mafia-connected produce dealer named Frank Liberto. Liberto, now deceased, had a courier deliver $100,000 for Jowers to hold at his restaurant, Jim's Grill, the back door of which opened onto the dense bushes across from the Lorraine Motel. Jowers said he was

visited the day before the murder by a man named Raul, who brought a rifle in a box.

The jury also heard a tape recording of a two-hour-long confession Jowers made at a fall 1998 meeting with Martin Luther King's son Dexter and former UN Ambassador Andrew Young.

On the tape Jowers says that meetings to plan the assassination occurred at Jim's Grill. He said planners included undercover Memphis Police Department officer Marrell McCollough (who now works for the Central Intelligence Agency, and who is referenced in the trial transcript as Merrell McCullough), MPD Lieutenant Earl Clark (who died in 1987), a third police officer, and two men Jowers did not know but thought were federal agents.

Jowers says on the tape that right after the shot was fired he received a smoking rifle at the rear door of Jim's Grill from Clark. He broke the rifle down into two pieces and wrapped it in a tablecloth. Raul picked it up the next day. Jowers said he didn't actually see who fired the shot that killed King, but thought it was Clark, the MPD's best marksman.

—The Martin Luther King Conspiracy Exposed in Memphis, Jim
Douglass, Probe Magazine.

During the trial some troubling facts came out about the lack of security that Dr. King had received in the hours leading up to his assassination.

On the night of April 3, 1968, Floyd E. Newsum, a black firefighter and civil rights activist, heard King's "I've Been to the Mountain Top" speech at the Mason Temple in Memphis. Newsum returned a phone call from his lieutenant and was told he had been temporarily transferred from Fire Station 2, located across the street from the Lorraine Motel…

The only other Black firefighter at Fire Station 2, Norvell E. Wallace, testified that he, too, received orders from his superior officer on the night of April 3 for a temporary transfer to a fire station far removed from the Lorraine Motel.

In a March-April Probe magazine article, Mike Vinson described the similar removal of Ed Redditt, a black Memphis Police Department detective, from *his* Fire Station 2 surveillance post two hours before King's murder.

Redditt testified at trial that when King's party and the police accompanying them arrived from the airport at the Lorraine Motel on April 3, he "noticed something that was unusual." When Inspector Don Smith, who was in charge of security, told Redditt he could leave, Redditt noticed there was nobody else there. "In the past when we were assigned to Dr. King we stayed with him. I saw nobody with him. So, I went across the street and asked the Fire Department could we come in and observe from the rear, which we did."

Redditt testified that late in the afternoon of April 4, MPD Intelligence Officer Eli Arkin came to Fire Station 2 to take him to Central Headquarters. There Police and Fire Director Frank Holloman, an FBI agent who had worked for the FBI for five years, and seven years as supervisor of J. Edgar Hoover's office) ordered Redditt home, against his wishes.

Former MPD Captain Jerry Williams followed Redditt to the witness stand.

Williams had been responsible for forming a special security unit of Black officers whenever King came to Memphis (the unit Redditt had served on earlier). Williams took pride in providing the best possible protection for Dr. King, which included, advising him never to stay at the Lorraine "because we couldn't furnish proper security there. It was just an open view of the hotel. To him it was a setup from the beginning, he told the court. There was no protection at-all."

For King's April 3, 1968 arrival, however, Williams was for some reason not asked to form the special black bodyguards. He was told years later by his inspector (a man whom Jowers identified as a participant in the meetings at Jim's Grill) that the change occurred because somebody in King's entourage had *asked,* specifically, for no

Black security officers. Williams told the judge and jury that the events that occurred that day, bothered him, "even to this day."

Leon Cohen, a retired New York City police officer, testified that in 1968 he had become friendly with the Lorraine Motel's owner and manager, Walter Bailey (now deceased). On the morning after King's murder, Cohen spoke with a visibly upset Bailey outside his office at the Lorraine. Bailey told Cohen about a strange request that had forced him to change King's room to the location where he was shot.

Bailey explained that the night before King's arrival he had received a call "from a member of Dr. King's group in Atlanta." The caller (whom Bailey said he knew but referred to only by the pronoun "he") wanted the motel owner to change King's room. Bailey said he was adamantly opposed to moving King, as instructed, from an inner court room behind the motel office (which had better security) to an outside balcony room exposed to public view.

—The Martin Luther King Conspiracy Exposed in Memphis, Jim Douglass, Probe Magazine.

A New York Times reporter staying at the Lorraine Motel at the time of Kings Assassination had stated in a video testimony that he had heard what he thought to be a bomb blast at 6:00 PM. When he looked outside the door, he said he saw a man crouching in bushes across the street, and that the man was staring at the Lorraine's balcony. The reporter wrote about what he had seen in an article; but was never questioned by law officials.

Another witness to the shooting (whose story never reached the public) was SCLC official James Orange, whose testimony was read into evidence at the trial.

"After the shot… I looked back and saw the smoke. It couldn't have been more than five to ten seconds. The smoke came out of the brush area on the opposite side of the street from the Lorraine Motel. I saw it rise up from the bushes over there. From that day to this time, I have never had any doubt that the fatal shot, the bullet which ended Dr. King's life, was fired by a sniper concealed in the brush area behind the derelict buildings."

Within hours of King's murder, the bushy area near the Loraine Motel, a potential crime scene, by orders of the police, was cleared of bushes, and debris. A Memphis Sanitation Department official testified that a call from Memphis Police Department had ordered that the brush in the vacant lot in the vicinity of the assassination be cut down immediately.

The evidence presented at the Civil Trail in 1999 was now pointing the finger not only at Jowers and the U.S. Government, but, also, at the U.S. Army—who had a sniper team in place, when King was gunned down.

Carthel Weeden, captain of Fire Station 2 in 1968, testified that he was on duty the morning of April 4 when two U.S. Army officers approached him. The officers said they wanted a lookout for the Lorraine Motel. Weeden said they carried briefcases and indicated they had cameras. Weeden showed the officers to the roof of the fire station. He left them at the edge of its northeast corner behind a parapet wall. From there the Army officers had a bird's-eye view of Dr. King's balcony doorway and could also look down on the brushy area adjacent to the fire station.
—The Martin Luther King Conspiracy Exposed in Memphis, Jim Douglass, Probe Magazine.

The civil suit against Lloyd Jowers, and the U.S. Government, had unearthed some rather startling revelations; and now, the jury, would have the following evidence to consider:

US 111th Military Intelligence Group were at Dr. King's location during the assassination.

20th Special Forces Group had an 8-man sniper team at the assassination location on that day.

Usual Memphis Police special body guards were advised they "weren't needed" on the day of the assassination.

Regular and constant police protection for Dr. King was removed from protecting Dr. King an hour before the assassination.

Military Intelligence set-up photographers on the roof of a fire station with clear view to Dr. King's balcony.

Dr. King's room was changed from a secure 1st-floor room to an exposed balcony room.

Memphis police ordered the scene that multiple witnesses reported as the source of shooting cut down, bushes that could have hid a sniper.

Along with sanitizing a crime scene, police abandoned investigative procedure to interview witnesses who lived by the scene of the shooting.

The rifle Mr. Ray delivered was not matched to the bullet that killed Dr. King, and was not sighted to accurately shoot.

And on December 8, 1999 the jury empaneled to decide if Bowers and the U.S. Government were indeed liable for the death of Dr. King, had reached a verdict:

"In answer to the question, 'Did Loyd Jowers participate in a conspiracy to do harm to Dr. Martin Luther King?' your answer is 'Yes.'"

The judge continued: "Do you also find that others, including governmental agencies, were parties to this conspiracy as alleged by the defendant? Your answer to that one is also 'Yes.'"

David Morphy, the only juror to grant an interview, said later: …"Everything from the police department being pulled back, to the death threat on Redditt, to the two black firefighters being pulled off, to the military people going up on top of the fire station, even to them going back to that point and cutting down the trees. Who in their right mind would go and destroy a crime scene like that the morning after? It was just very, very odd."

Dexter King, the plaintiffs' final witness, said the trial was about why his father had been killed: "It is not about who killed Martin Luther King Jr., my father. It is not necessarily about all of those details. It is about: Why was he killed? Because if you answer the why, you will understand the same things are still happening. Until we address that, we're all in trouble. Because if it could happen to him, if it can happen to this family, it can happen to anybody."

"It is so amazing for me that as soon as this issue of potential involvement of the federal government came up, all of a sudden the media just went totally negative against the family. I couldn't understand that. I kept asking my mother, 'What is going on?'"

"She reminded me," she said. "Dexter, your dad and I have lived through this once already. You have to understand that when you take a stand against the establishment, first, you will be attacked. There is an attempt to discredit. Second, [an attempt] to try and character-assassinate. And third, ultimately physical termination or assassination."

"Now the truth of the matter is if my father had stopped and not spoken out, if he had just somehow compromised, he would probably still be here with us today. But the minute you start talking about redistribution of wealth and stopping a major conflict, which also has economic ramifications...?"

—The Martin Luther King Conspiracy Exposed in Memphis,
Jim Douglass, Probe Magazine.

Perhaps the most bizarre aspect of this history making verdict, is the fact that the corporate owned U.S. media chose to turn blind eyes to the trial itself and to its findings. Journalist and author James Douglass, who covered the trial from beginning to end, had this to say about the absence of a strangely incurious media.

"I can hardly believe the fact that, apart from the courtroom participants, only Memphis TV reporter Wendell Stacy and I attended from beginning to end this historic three-and-one-half week trial.

Because of journalistic neglect scarcely anyone else in this land of ours even knows what went on in it."

Throughout the 1970s, the FBI continued its take-no-prisoners, all-out assault against the leaders of the Civil Rights Movement:

Hoover's Men in Black had used methods of infiltration, legal harassment, psychological warfare, and entrapment, to subdue, and annihilate almost the entire Civil Rights Movement. Unscrupulous agents had used police departments throughout the country to raid the homes of suspected militants with little or no evidence, and had framed many others on trumped up charges that landed them behind bars for extraordinarily long periods of time.

And so: as the 1970s came and went, it is here that we see a noticeable change in the air, a downsizing, a disheartening abandonment of the ideas that the Civil Rights Movement had been founded upon. And now, because of internal conflict between opposing philosophies and because of outside intervention—on the part of the FBI and other law enforcement agencies—the Movement was brought to its knees; and the upward mobility of the entire Black race... was now in danger of being completely eradicated.

Chapter Four
Plantation Social Engineering

"I never will forget it: how my master always used to say, 'Keep a nigger down.' I never will forget it. I used to wait on tables and I heard them talk."
—Hannah Davidson, former slave, interviewed in the 1930s by the WPA.

President Ronald Reagan, in his fatherly speech to the nation on February 14, 1986, with smiling Nancy at his side, said, in a tone eerily similar to the tone that had been used by Harry Anslinger, in his war against the Negro scourge marijuana, decades earlier:

"Drugs are menacing our society! They're killing our children… From the beginning of our administration, we've taken strong steps to do something about this horror. Tonight I can report to you that we've made much progress. Thirty-seven federal agencies are working together in a vigorous national effort. And by next year our spending for drug enforcement will have tripled… But despite our best efforts, illegal cocaine is coming into our country at alarming levels… Today, there's a new epidemic: Smokable cocaine, otherwise known as Crack. It is an explosively destructive and often lethal substance which is crushing its users. It is an uncontrolled fire. And drug abuse is not a so-called victimless crime. Everyone's safety is at stake…"

And the *game* was on.

And just as the Hearst newspapers in the 1890s sprang into action warning America about the Yellow Opium Menace, and just as movie newsreels in the 1930s showed in graphic detail the ravaging effects of Killer Marijuana Menace, now, in the 1980s, newspapers, and TV stations all across America marched robotically into action, describing the newest Negro Menace, that had been disguised to look like the newest Crack Cocaine Menace.

And as America went into panic mode concerning the latest *drug* menace… in the jungles of Nicaragua, cargo planes operated by the CIA (loaded with cocaine) were motoring down wooded airstrips bound for America. A war was being waged, but that war was not a war on drugs. It was a war against the leftist Nicaraguan rebels.

To finance that war, a war Congress refused to finance, plane loads of cash was needed; and needed desperately.

Oliver North, a Marine lieutenant colonel made national headlines when it was learned that airplanes under his direction had been used to transport so-called *humanitarian aid* to the Contras in South America. But the shocking part of the story was that those same planes were being used to transport drugs into *North* America.

Linking North to the covert operation was an email that he received on February 10, 1986, discussing a plane that had been used to carry "humanitarian aid" to the contras that had been used previously to transport drugs. The plane's owner was Michael Palmer, one of the largest marijuana smugglers in the country. Palmer had a long history of drug smuggling, but he had been awarded over $300,000.00 from the Nicaraguan Humanitarian Aid Office, run by Oliver North, to ship humanitarian supplies to the contras.

But what was not known by the American people was that as Nancy Reagan traveled from state-to-state preaching just say no, her husband's administration with its fingerprints on the illegal war in Nicaragua was saying yes, yes, to more secretly imported drugs being shipped into the Black ghettos of America.

And no one would come out a bigger winner, in this new-found world of prosperity, than Freeway Ricky Ross.

In less than three years Ricky Ross would give up a life of poverty, and would step into a gleaming world of unimaginable wealth and luxury—almost overnight, he would find himself swimming in *cash.*

I found myself on the streets of South-Central Los Angeles. So I'm walking around; trying to figure out what I'm go do with myself. Couldn't [find] a job… Anything I could make a living I was willing… One of my friends came from college. And he had this stuff called cocaine. I can remember that before I started selling cocaine, they started coming out with movies like Superfly. Almost like priming you for this new lifestyle that you're about to get into. So, when the friend showed me the cocaine, I thought of Superfly. I was interested, because I had saw Superfly. My friend shows me this stuff. It's yellowish white. I'm like, I thought cocaine was supposed to be white. So he gives me fifty dollars' worth. He says, go and see what you can do with it. So, I go around the neighborhood, I'm asking everybody. But nobody knows what it is. Finally, I run into a pimp. And he says, let me see it. And he takes it and he cooks it up, and he says, oh yes, it's pretty good stuff… And that's how I got started selling cocaine… This one person would come and buy from me, and then another one would come, and he would introduce me to somebody else, until some days I'm making three million dollars a day.

—Freeway Ricky Ross.

Ross later would be introduced to a Nicaraguan exile named Danillo Blandon. The CIA connected Blando agreed to supply the neophyte drug-pusher with choice cocaine much cheaper than the average street price, and sweetening the pot, Ross would be allowed take the drugs on consignment and would pay when he was paid.

And suddenly a drug that no one knew about had become the drug of choice in inner cities throughout the country.

But Freeway Ricky Ross had no way of knowing, that he was secretly working, for the CIA…

He had no way of knowing that the proceeds from this nation-wide drug smuggling operation were being funneled straight into the revolution against the Sandinista rulers in Nicaragua, the arch enemy of the U.S. backed Contra rebels.

So successful was this new alliance between the South American rebels and a South Los Angeles high school dropout, that Ross was able to pump staggering amounts of cocaine not just throughout the city of Los Angeles, but into Kansas City, Oklahoma, St. Louis, Seattle, and as far away as New York City on the opposite Coast.

In a scant few years Freeway Ricky Ross would become the stuff of which legends are made.

But with duffel bags of cash suddenly flowing into the poverty-stricken South Central area of the city, the Los Angeles Police was bound to turn its attention from jaywalkers to the upstart young drug pusher sooner or later: who hadn't had the foresight to bribe his overlords; the police department. And it would be this *oversight*, this *failure* to pay tribute where tribute was required, that would be his downfall.

In January of 1987 the L.A.P.D. would form a task force, targeting Ricky Ross, and other known drug dealers in and around the South Central Los Angeles district. The crew consisting of nine carefully chosen police officers was quickly assembled. And now free of sufficient oversight the crew that would come to be known as the Freeway Ricky Task Force was on its way to becoming a law unto itself: A band of renegade cops.

Adapting an anything-goes attitude in their over-zealous efforts to snare the elusive Ricky Ross they themselves would be indicted in later years for the very crimes they had hoped to bring against Ross. They had planted cocaine. They had conjured up one phony charge after another and none had stuck. Ross would eventually be arrested, but the charges would be dismissed when the cops close to the investigation would have charges of corruption brought against them.

Finally, on June 8 of 1989, Ross would be charged with conspiring to distribute cocaine into the city of Cincinnati. And although Ross would later claim that he had been set up by the cops, at last, it looked as if the rags-to-riches young drugster was on his way to the Big Slammer.

But at that moment, the police were not the only ones who were trailing young Ricky Ross' every step. A journalist, named Gary Webb, was on his trail as well.

[Gary] told me he was going to get to the bottom of it. He did tell me about a new book he was working on. And he asked me if I would be a part of that.

—Freeway Ricky Ross.

An investigative reporter for the San Jose Mercury News, Webb had won numerous awards for his work; and now, he was on the scent of a story that some journalist would kill for, a story, that he might actually have died for.

When that once in a lifetime scoop appeared in the San Jose Mercury News, in 1996, its lead paragraph was as explosive as a stick of dynamite:

An investigation by the Mercury News had found that for the better part of a decade, a highly financed drug-ring, had sold tons of cocaine to the Crips and Bloods street gangs of Los Angeles, and funneled millions in drug profits to a Latin American guerrilla army run by the U.S. Central Intelligence Agency: A drug network that had opened the first pipeline between Colombia's cocaine cartels and the Black neighborhoods of Los Angeles, a city that would become known as the crack capital of the world.

The lid had been lifted off the pot: The U.S. Government's role in a major drug trafficking ring had been exposed.

But Webb's bombshell would be roundly condemned by reputable newspapers across the country for its so-called lack of sufficient evidence.

Webb, as far as the national media was concerned, was just another conspiracy nut with an axe to grind. But the story was gaining traction over the Internet, and was growing rapidly into a national scandal.

The night that I read [Webb's] 'Dark Alliance' series, I was so alarmed, that I literally sat straight up in bed, poring over every word. I reflected on the many meetings I attended throughout South Central Los Angeles during the 1980s, when I constantly asked, 'Where are all the drugs coming from?' I asked myself that night whether it was possible for such a vast amount of drugs to be smuggled into any district under the noses of the community leaders, police, sheriff's department, FBI, DEA and other law enforcement agencies...

The time I spent investigating the allegations of the 'Dark Alliance' series led me to the undeniable conclusion that the CIA, DEA, DIA, and FBI knew about drug trafficking in South Central Los Angeles. They were either part of the trafficking or turned a blind eye to it, [in] an effort to fund the Contra war.

—Congresswoman Maxine Waters.

On December 10, 2004, Gary Webb was found dead in his home—two bullets pumped into his head—the victim of a suicide.

But had he managed to shoot himself in the head, twice, or, did he receive a friendly assist from unknown quarters?

If we had met five years ago, you wouldn't have found a more staunch defender of the newspaper industry than me... And then I wrote some stories that made me realize how sadly misplaced my

bliss had been. The reason I'd enjoyed such smooth sailing for so long hadn't been, as I'd assumed, because I was careful and diligent and good at my job... The truth was that, in all those years, I hadn't written anything important enough to suppress.

—Gary Webb.

Senator John Kerry, chairman of a two-and-a-half-year investigation into Terrorism, Narcotics, and International Operations, said: "It is clear that individuals who provided support for the Contras were involved in drug trafficking...and elements of the Contras themselves knowingly received financial and material assistance from drug traffickers."

Gary Webb had learned the hard way that it is not nice to provoke Ol Massa. In life he was roundly condemned as a nut-case, a chaser of conspiracy theories, and even in death so-called reputable newspapers to this day uptick their defense of the Criminals, while crucifying the memory of the Messenger.

"It may take time, but I am convinced that history is going to record that Gary Webb wrote the truth. The establishment refused to give Gary Webb the credit that he deserved. They teamed up in an effort to destroy the story—and very nearly succeeded... We will not let this story end until the naysayers and opponents are forced to apologize for their reckless and irresponsible attacks on Gary Webb."

—Congresswoman Maxine Waters.

How much of an impact did this one drug have on the future of Black America?

William N. Evans of Notre Dame, Craig Garthwaite of Northwestern and Timothy J. Moore of George Washington University concluded that the differences in high school graduation rates and standardized test scores of white and black students [had] narrowed between the mid-

1960s and the late 1980s, as the educational outcomes of black students improved significantly.

"We propose the rise of crack cocaine markets as an explanation for the end to the convergence in black-white educational outcomes beginning in the mid-1980s. After constructing a measure to date the arrival of crack markets in cities and states, we show large increases in murder and incarceration rates after these dates. Black high school graduation rates also decline, and we estimate that crack markets accounts for between 40 and 73 percent of the fall in black male high school graduation rates."

After decades of decline, black infant mortality soared to record levels in the 1980s, as did the rate of low-birth weight babies and parent abandonment. The gap between black and white schoolchildren widened. The number of blacks sent to prison tripled. Future progress was not only stopped cold but was often knocked as much as ten years backward. And Black Americans were hurt more by crack cocaine than by any other single cause since Jim Crow.

Within a five-year time period, the homicide rate among young urban Blacks, had quadrupled.

Black kids growing up in ghettos infested with crack cocaine—like calves born to wildebeests in Africa—grew up quickly. And on the run.

Young Black males had little time to weep for the endangered whale, or the endangered tiger, when he himself was on someone's menu; and was on his own endangered species list. His chances of being murdered, or incarcerated, were spiraling off the charts suddenly. Many had witnessed killings, drugs transactions and drive-by shootings in their baby years. And carrying a gun by the age of ten, in some parts of town, were parentally encouraged.

Crack cocaine had not only impeded the progress the Black race had made prior to the 1980s, it also had managed to *socially engineer* the Black race to the point that it was primed and ready: for Ol Massa's greatest schemes of all.

Chapter Five
The Gangsta Plantation

An anonymous letter mysteriously appeared on the Internet a few years ago: And created a firestorm.

No one knows to this day if the letter is true or false. For that reason, it is presented here un-revised, and un-edited, and the reader is left to make up his or her own mind as to whether it is *fact*, or *fiction*, disguised as fact.

Hello:

After more than 20 years, I've finally decided to tell the world what I witnessed in 1991, which I believe was one of the biggest turning point in popular music, and ultimately American society. I have struggled for a long time weighing the pros and cons of making this story public as I was reluctant to implicate the individuals who were present that day. So I've simply decided to leave out names and all the details that may risk my personal well-being and that of those who were, like me, dragged into something they weren't ready for.

Between the late '80s and early '90s, I was what you may call a "decision maker" with one of the more established company in the music industry. I came from Europe in the early '80s and quickly established myself in the business. The industry was different back then. Since technology and media weren't accessible to people like they are today, the industry had more control over the public and had the means to influence them anyway it wanted. This may

explain why in early 1991, I was invited to attend a closed door meeting with a small group of music business insiders to discuss rap music's new direction. Little did I know that we would be asked to participate in one of the most unethical and destructive business practice I've ever seen.

The meeting was held at a private residence on the outskirts of Los Angeles. I remember about 25 to 30 people being there, most of them familiar faces. Speaking to those I knew, we joked about the theme of the meeting as many of us did not care for rap music and failed to see the purpose of being invited to a private gathering to discuss its future. Among the attendees was a small group of unfamiliar faces who stayed to themselves and made no attempt to socialize beyond their circle. Based on their behavior and formal appearances, they didn't seem to be in our industry. Our casual chatter was interrupted when we were asked to sign a confidentiality agreement preventing us from publicly discussing the information presented during the meeting. Needless to say, this intrigued and in some cases disturbed many of us. The agreement was only a page long but very clear on the matter and consequences which stated that violating the terms would result in job termination. We asked several people what this meeting was about and the reason for such secrecy but couldn't find anyone who had answers for us. A few people refused to sign and walked out. No one stopped them. I was tempted to follow but curiosity got the best of me. A man who was part of the "unfamiliar" group collected the agreements from us.

Quickly after the meeting began, one of my industry colleagues (who shall remain nameless like everyone else) thanked us for attending. He then gave the floor to a man who only introduced himself by first name and gave no further details about his personal background. I think he was the owner of the residence but it was never confirmed. He briefly praised all of us for the success we had achieved in our industry and congratulated us for being selected as part of this small group of 'decision makers'. At this point I begin to feel slightly uncomfortable at the strangeness of this gathering. The subject quickly changed as the speaker went on to tell us that the respective companies we represented had invested in a very profitable industry which could become even more rewarding with our active involvement. He explained that the companies we work for had invested millions into the building of privately owned prisons and that our positions of influence in the music industry would actually impact the profitability of these investments. I remember many of us in the group immediately looking at each other in confusion. At the time, I didn't know what a private prison was but I wasn't the only one. Sure enough, someone asked what these prisons were and what any of this had to do with us. We were told that these prisons were built by privately owned companies who received funding from the government based on the number of inmates. The more inmates, the more money the government would pay these prisons. It was also made clear to us that since these prisons are privately owned, as they become publicly traded, we'd be able to buy shares. Most of us were taken back by this. Again, a couple of people asked what this had to do with us. At this point, my industry colleague who had first opened the meeting took the floor again and answered our questions. He told us that since our employers had become silent investors in this prison business, it was now in their interest to make sure that these prisons remained filled. Our job would be to help make this happen by marketing music which promotes criminal behavior, rap being the music of choice. He assured us that this would be a great situation for us because rap music was becoming an increasingly profitable market for our companies, and as employee, we'd also be able to buy personal stocks in these prisons. Immediately, silence came over the room. You could have heard a pin drop. I remember looking around to make sure I wasn't dreaming and saw half of the people with dropped jaws. My daze was interrupted when someone shouted, "Is this a f****** joke?" At this point things became chaotic. Two of the men who were part of the "unfamiliar" group grabbed the man who shouted out and attempted to remove him from the house. A few of us, myself included, tried to intervene. One of them pulled out a gun and we all backed off. They separated us from the crowd and all four of us were escorted outside. My industry colleague who had opened the meeting earlier hurried out to meet us and reminded us that we had signed agreement and would suffer the consequences of speaking about this publicly or even with those who attended the meeting. I asked him why he was involved with something this corrupt and he replied that it was bigger than the music business and nothing we'd want to challenge without risking consequences. We all protested and as he walked back into the house I remember word for word the last thing he said, "It's out of my hands now. Remember you signed an agreement." He then closed the door behind him. The men rushed us to our cars and actually watched until we drove off.

A million things were going through my mind as I drove away and I eventually decided to pull over and park on a side street in order to collect my thoughts. I replayed everything in my mind repeatedly and it all seemed very surreal to me. I was angry with myself for not having taken a more active role in questioning what had been presented to us. I'd like to believe the shock of it all is what suspended my better nature.

After what seemed like an eternity, I was able to calm myself enough to make it home. I didn't talk or call anyone that night. The next day back at the office, I was visibly out of it but blamed it on being under the weather. No one else in my department had been invited to the meeting and I felt a sense of guilt for not being able to share what I had witnessed. I thought about contacting the three others who wear kicked out of the house but I didn't remember their names and thought that tracking them down would probably bring unwanted attention. I considered speaking out publicly at the risk of losing my job but I realized I'd probably be jeopardizing more than my job and I wasn't willing to risk anything happening to my family. I thought about those men with guns and wondered who they were? I had been told that this was bigger than the music business and all I could do was let my imagination run free. There were no answers and no one to talk to. I tried to do a little bit of research on private prisons but didn't uncover anything about the music business' involvement. However, the information I did find confirmed how dangerous this prison business really was. Days turned into weeks and weeks into months. Eventually, it was as if the meeting had never taken place. It all seemed surreal. I became more reclusive and stopped going to any industry events unless professionally obligated to do so. On two occasions, I found myself attending the same function as my former colleague. Both times, our eyes met but nothing more was exchanged.

As the months passed, rap music had definitely changed direction. I was never a fan of it but even I could tell the difference. Rap acts that talked about politics or harmless fun were quickly fading away as gangster rap started dominating the airwaves. Only a few months had passed since the meeting but I suspect that the ideas presented that day had been successfully implemented. It was as if the order has been given to all major label executives. The music was climbing the charts and most companies when more than happy to capitalize on it. Each one was churning out their very own gangster rap acts on an assembly line. Everyone bought into it, consumers included. Violence and drug use became a central theme in most rap music. I spoke to a few of my peers in the industry to get their opinions on the new trend but was told repeatedly that it was all about supply and demand. Sadly many of them even expressed that the music reinforced their prejudice of minorities.

I officially quit the music business in 1993 but my heart had already left months before. I broke ties with the majority of my peers and removed myself from this thing I had once loved. I took some time off, returned to Europe for a few years, settled out of state, and lived a "quiet" life away from the world of entertainment. As the years passed, I managed to keep my secret, fearful of sharing it with the wrong person but also a little ashamed of not having had the balls to blow the whistle. But as rap got worse, my guilt grew. Fortunately, in the late 90s, having the internet as a resource which wasn't at my disposal in the early days made it easier for me to investigate what is now labeled the prison industrial complex.

Now that I have a greater understanding of how private prisons operate, things make much more sense than they ever have. I see how the criminalization of rap music played a big part in promoting racial stereotypes and misguided so many impressionable young minds into adopting these glorified criminal behaviors which often lead to incarceration. Twenty years of guilt is a heavy load to carry but the least I can do now is to share my story, hoping that fans of rap music realize how they've been used for the past two decades. Although I plan on remaining anonymous for obvious reasons, my goal now is to get this information out to as many people as possible. Please help me spread the word. Hopefully, others who attended the meeting back in 1991 will be inspired by this and tell their own stories. Most importantly, if only one life has been touched by my story, I pray it makes the weight of my guilt a little more tolerable.

Thank you.

Fact, or fiction disguised as fact. Who knows?

But what *is* known is that rap-record companies—propagating and profiting from a thuggish, hip-hop culture that they helped to invent— were directly linked to corporations that own, and operate private prisons. That: *is* a fact.

"Tell the bitches that be hatin' I ain't got no worries.
I just wanna hit and run like I ain't got insurance.
aHoe what's yo name what's yo sign zodiac killer.

All rats gotta die even master splinter yea.
Murder 187. I be killin' them bitches.
I hope all dogs go to heaven.
And I got xanax, percocet, promethazine with codine.
Call me Mr. Sand Man, I'm selling all these hoe's dreams"

—Lil Wayne.

Lil Wayne's brotherhood-advocating, race-uplifting lyrics were produced by Cash Money Records, and distributed by Republic Records. Republic Records operated as a division of Universal Music Group, owned by General Electric. And General Electric, until recently, was heavily invested in what?—the private prison industry.

"Leave a bitch nigga head in pasta. You are an imposter, ain't got no money. Put the burner to his tummy, and make it bubbly. I really hate niggas I'm a Nazi."

—Def Loaf.

Mr. Def Loaf's insightful commentary about what it takes to be a Black man in today's world, is money in the bank for Mr. Def, and Black butts in prisons, for his corporate sponsors.

A true friend of the Black race Mr. Def seems to be Ol Massa' shining achievement: A Negro, who actively participates in his own, ignominious—but well-deserved—destruction.

Prison generating messages of this sort is like plucking money from trees for a growing list of Major Corporations—who obviously know a good, nappy-headed *thing*...

When they *see* him?

Viacom and AOL Time Warner, and a host of other billion-dollar multi-media corporations, have also invested heavily in private prisons, raking in loot from young wannabe thugs that *they* create, and then harvest like wild-eyed money-sprouting vegetables, that just keeps on growing.

Chapter Six
Plantation Private Prisons

Statistics show that from 1970 to 2005, the population in prisons increased 700 percent—as violent crimes declined—giving America the dubious distinction of having the highest incarceration rate in the world. For the least amount of crime? And the private prison establishment would like to keep it that way. They have lobbied and bribed Congress for stiffer and longer drug sentencing, stating:

"The demand for our facilities and services could be adversely affected by the relaxation of enforcement efforts, leniency in conviction or parole standards and sentencing practices or through the decriminalization of certain activities that are currently proscribed by our criminal laws. For instance, any changes with respect to drugs and controlled substances or illegal immigration could affect the number of persons arrested, convicted, and sentenced, thereby potentially reducing demand for correctional facilities to house them."

Jamie Fellner, associated counsel of Human Rights Watch says that five times as many whites use drugs than Blacks, but that:

* Nationwide, black men are sent to state prison on drug charges at 13 times the rate of white men.
* Black men are incarcerated at 9.6 times the rate of white men. In eleven states, they are incarcerated at rates that are 12 to 26 times greater than that of white men.
* Nationwide, one in every 20 Black men over the age of 18 is in prison.

Ecstatically satisfied with these golden numbers the CEO of Corrections Corporation of America, Damon Hiniger, in a press release said:

"We are pleased our populations have remained strong, in excess of the 80,000 inmate milestone we surpassed late in 2010. With the 3.2% increase in inmate population over the previous year, Corrections Corp. of America was able to make $511.26M profit, earning their CEO over $3,000,000 in compensation."

Today, companies like Motorola, AT@T, Texas Instruments, Dell, IBM, Honeywell, Boeing, Noriel, Target Stores, Macy's and TWA, and a host of others, have profited, or still profits, from prison labor.

Therefore it should come as no surprise to anyone that companies that once paid 20 dollars per hour, union-scale, are now paying 25 cents per hour, convict-scale.

...Today's corporations can lease factories in prisons, as well as lease prisoners out to their factories.

And in the most extreme cases, we are even witnessing the reemergence of the chain gang.

"In Arizona, the self-proclaimed 'toughest sheriff in America', Joe Arpaio, requires his Maricopa County inmates to enroll in chain gangs to perform various community services or face lockdown with three other inmates in an 8×12-foot cell, for 23 hours a day. In June of this year, Arpaio started a female-only chain gang made up of women convicted of driving under the influence. In a press release

he boasted that the inmates would be wearing pink T—shirts emblazoned with the message about drinking and driving."

—21st Century Slaves: How Corporations Exploit Prison Labor,

Khalet goes on to say that: "In 2008, over 2.3 million Americans were in prison or jail, with one of every 48 working-age men behind bars… That doesn't include the tens of thousands of detained undocumented immigrants facing deportation, prisoners awaiting sentencing, or juveniles caught up in the school-to-prison pipeline."

Stephen Harnet in his book, Prison Labor, Slavery & Capitalism in Historical Perspective says, "We now are witnessing the production of a correctional-industrial complex in which society's already limited resources and funds are redistributed away from social justice-based forms of spending, in favor of imprisonment."

"As an example, he says that while we are cutting spending on education, housing, health care, and other long-term infrastructural necessities, the Bureau of Justice Statistics reports that state spending on prison construction increased 612% between 1979 and 1990. The American Friends Service Committee characterizes this redistribution of wealth, resources, and possibilities as part of an oncoming 'fortress economy' in which an America ever more stratified by racial and class divisions retreats into armed enclaves where the promises and obligations of justice and democracy are increasingly replaced by a high-tech correctional-industrial police state."

Private prisons have had a devastating effect on almost every aspect of society, but no one should really be surprised by its insidious over-reach or its sudden appearance. The use of convict labor is as old as America; for it dates back to pre-Colonial times.

…It is important to recall that many of the first settlers of the "New World" were actually British, Scottish, Irish, French, German, and Dutch convicts sold into indentured servitude…

{This} enabled the traditional elite to rid themselves of potential political radicals, and provided the cheap labor necessary for the first wave of colonization. Indeed, as detailed in both Peter Linebaugh's The London Hanged and A. R. Ekirch's Bound for America, there is a strong historical relationship between the need for policing the unruly working classes, fueling the military and economic needs of the capitalist class, and greasing the wheels of imperialism with both indentured servants and outright slavery.

—Stephen Harnett, Prison Labor, Slavery @ Capitalism in Historical
Perspective.

Is anyone *surprised* that there are now more than half a million inmates working full-time in jails and prisons, in America?

Bad behavior and high unemployment rates have always translated into high incarcerations rates. And high incarcerations, in today's world, translates into more private prisons, and *more* private prisons under the guise of rehabilitation require *more* and *more* incarcerations, and more and more incarcerations, requires more and more Black butts… to be station near or on, the Old Plantation?

The old-time prison-labor exploiters, who colonized early America, must be smiling in their devilish graves. Their blueprint—is *working*—to *perfection*.

Working to perfection to such a degree that South Carolina State Rep. Bill Chumley (R) has sponsored a bill that would shackle low-level plantation inductees into modern-day chain gangs. "We have *miles* and *miles* of highway that need things *done* to them," Chumley [cracking his bullwhip] has said, in television interviews.

Meanwhile, the march toward the complete privatization of America's prisons continues, at a frantic pace.

I'm a boss ass bitch, bitch, bitch, bitch, bitch, bitch, bitch
I'm a boss ass bitch, bitch, bitch, bitch, bitch, bitch, bitch
I'm a boss ass bitch, bitch, bitch, bitch, bitch, bitch, bitch

I'm a boss ass bitch, bitch, bitch, bitch, bitch, bitch, bitch!

Nicki Manaj, BET Award Winner, Female Singer.

Fortunately, for her, the Pied Piper Miss Nicki, will be nowhere to be found when her young imitators turn around in their prison cells, and find themselves staring up at a towering six-foot-seven convict, named Big Bertha. And when her young disciples tell Bertha that they are a bitch, a bitch, a bitch, a boss bitch! Bertha will be pleased. Very, very *pleased*. Not as pleased as the rap-recording companies, who invest in private prisons, not as pleased as racist white judges who get their kicks kicking any stray Black butt they can round up, and lock up—not as pleased as Ol Massa, when the old fart settles back on his great white steed, and surveys his sprawling, insanely profitable private-prisons—but Bertha, as she settled down and does *her* thing, will be pleased, oh! She will be very, *very... pleased...*

If one listens, very closely, one can still hear the echoes of that long ago meeting in 1866, when Henry Grady, the editor of the Atlanta Constitution, spoke at a dinner attended by J. P. Morgan, and a cadre of other high-powered financiers:

"Let bygones be bygones, let us have a new era of peace and prosperity; the Negro was a prosperous laboring class; he had the fullest protection of the laws and the friendship of the southern people. Grady had joked about the northerners who sold slaves to the South and said the South could now handle its own race problem. And he received a rising ovation, as the band played 'Dixie'."

And the band is *still* playing Dixie—from a distinctly Southerly direction—as the socially engineered Negro steps up to the old auction block—to once again assume his rightful God-assigned place on this *new*, but very *old*, twenty-first century, *prison* plantation.

The journey… that we set upon… at the beginning of this book, has barely begun.

But the evidence presented thus far seems to strongly suggest—beyond a shadowy shade of a doubt—that, the very same forces that had worked behind the scenes to herd the master's slaves *back* into the cotton-fields *after* the Civil War, are still very much *alive*; and are doing quite well, and, are working full time behind and in front of the scenes at this very hour—to keep his twenty-first century Slave, drugged-down, thugged-down, and knocked totally *out*, on his odd-looking, but very familiar-looking, surroundings.

Ol Massa—who has not taken his eyes off of his former slaves long enough to go to the bathroom—is still up to his old tricks—it seems—and is still smiling, like a cat, with a mouthful of dumb, wide-eyed, Black rats.

Chapter Seven
Plantation Negro Preachers

Oh *yes* how sweet it would be, *if*, after reading the preceding chapters, we could all join hands and cry a river as we blame that Ol' Devil white man for keeping the poor helpless Black man *chained* to slavery in one form or another for the past ten thousand gazillion years, or *more*! Oh, the tears we could shed for all of that agony, all of that pain, all of the blood and the sweat and the tears inflicted on God's po' helpless defenseless chilluns! Oh mercy! Mercy! Mercy! Mercy me?

But; when all is said, and all is done? That old African proverb, you know the one that says, *if there is no enemy inside your home, the enemy outside can do you no harm*, yes, that one; it reminds us that it was Black African chieftains who sold their fellow Africans to that white Devil, in the bushes.

The plain fact of the matter is that that road that has led the Black race here to this ignominious moment in time leads us back to a host of villains: the white ones, we all know about; the Black ones we conveniently choose to ignore? But the starring villains in the *black* capes in this bleak one-horse opera, has been, and continues to be, Negro plantation-minded politicians (whose crimes are so numerous that they alone will take up an entire book) and Negro, you guessed it, plantation-minded preachers.

Martin Luther King famously said:

"I'd like somebody to mention that day that Martin Luther King Jr. tried to give his life serving others. I'd like for somebody to say that day that Martin Luther King Jr. tried to love somebody.

I want you to say that day that I tried to be right on the war question. I want you to be able to say that day that I did try to feed the hungry. I want you to be able to say that day that I did try in my life to clothe those who were naked. I want you to say on that day that I did try in my life to visit those who were in prison. And I want you to say that I tried to love and serve humanity.

Yes, if you want to say that I was a drum major. Say that I was a drum major for justice. Say that I was a drum major for peace. I was a drum major for righteousness. And all of the other shallow things will not matter. I won't have any money to leave behind. I won't have the fine and luxurious things of life to leave behind. But I just want to leave a committed life behind."

But was King's Drum Major battle-cry a lone cry in the wilderness?

And was *his*, the battle cry of all so-called Black leaders who followed in his wake?

Most notably, in the areas of politics, and religion, were King's wish to love and serve humanity, *shared* values, among all the so-called Black leaders within those separate but related fields of endeavor?

"A white preacher always told us to obey our masters and work hard and sing and when we die we go to Heaven. Marse Tom didn't mind us singin' in our cabins, at night, but we better not let him catch us prayin'."

—William Moore, former slave, WPA interviewed in the 1930s.

Stroll leisurely into any town in America—large or small—where there is a large or small population of Blacks, and black religious critics say that if you listen very carefully, you can still hear the whispers of dead, Ghostly Voices: selling their lowly, uneducated brethren down the river.

Listen, intently, they say… and you can hear *ghostly sell-outs,* speaking from their craven, smoldering graves…

"… Howdy, Reverend…"

" … Hi'dy Suh."

"Them rumors, I been hearin', they ain't true, now is they Rev?"

"Ru-Ru-Rumors, Suh…?"

"Rumors says yo' congregation is a might… up-set…?"

"Why naw-suh! Why we's as pleased, as pleased can be! Yassuh!"

"Rumor say, you folks is… hungry? You all want a… better life?"

"Hun-gry, yassuh, but happy. Happy in The Word, Suh."

"Powerfully pleased we be on the… same page, Preacher?"

"The same exact page, Suh. Oh the same, ex-act page, yas-suh!"

"You a credit to yo' race, Preacher, and you shall be rewarded."

"In the sky, bye-n-bye, yassuh."

"You sho' is a blessing to yo' people."

"Leadership, Suh. What my people need is slow, patient… leadership."

"And you gives it to them, in spades, Preacher. And to show my appreciation…"

"A gift, Suh, f-for me—! I mean, for the… church…?"

"A do-nation, to the… church…?"

"Ten dollars! And so un-expected! Suh—the congregation—is pleased…"

The Black preacher, black religious critics claim, was the first Black sell-out politician.

According to Kirk Byron Jones, in his essay, Black Preachers and Public Life:

"...The Black preachers served as a bridge between the black and white worlds... This ironic arrangement, in which the Black preacher represented the white community, had its roots in the slave master's use of slave preachers to deliver sermons espousing otherworldly realities. As time went on, the Black preacher became the white man's telephone to the Black community."

In other words: As the Black preacher was providing succor, and comfort, to his lambs, by preaching a pacifist philosophy, he was also providing peace, of mind, for Ol Massa.

The words: *insurrection, revolt, uprising,* and *murder in the night,* had sent cold shivers up and down the spines of white respectable society, in the South, *and,* in the North, *and* in the East, *and,* in the West. It was those *very* words, those pillaging, deflowering words... that made Ol' Massa sit up late, burning barrels, and barrels of midnight oil.

Black religious institutions have had a lot to do with how we've gotten into the position we're in, but I also believe that they have a lot to do with how we stay in the position we're in... A hundred years ago you could go to the church and it would help you get a job. You could go to the church if you had social issues. You could go to the church if you had run-ins with the law, if your rights were impeded upon. Unfortunately today, the Black church is only prepared to get people ready for Heaven. But they are totally content with allowing Black people to exist in political hell, every day.

—Dr. Umar Johnson, psychologist.

The first Black church in America was established in 1792 in Philadelphia Pennsylvania. The African Methodist Episcopal Church pastored by its founder Richard Allen provided education and marriage counseling, and, operated a charity for poor Blacks in Philadelphia.

Allen also led a very vigorous campaign against slavery, operating one of the earliest stops on the Underground Railroad.

The Black church in the years following Slavery would become the go-to place when trouble came knocking: The employment office, the help with the law, office, the councilor, office; the Black worshipper's rock, harbor, and haven. The Black church in other words would become the very backbone that held up an entire disenfranchised, and sometimes totally isolated, Black community.

Able to cross that great divide between the white man's world and his own world the Black preacher quickly found himself endowed with the ability to *do* for his people, or, to *do* for himself. And in far too many places and in far too many cases, they chose to *do…* for themselves.

"First, we must realize that no such institution as the Negro church could rear itself without definite historical foundations. These foundations we can find if we remember that the social history of the Negro did not start in America. He was brought from a definite social environment,—the polygamous clan life under the headship of the chief and the potent influence of the priest. His religion was nature-worship, with profound belief in invisible surrounding influences good and bad, and his worship was through incantation and sacrifice. The first rude change in this life was the slave ship and the West Indian sugar-fields. The plantation organization replaced the clan and tribe, and the white master replaced the chief with far greater and more despotic powers. Forced and long-continued toil became the rule of life, the old ties of blood relationship and kinship disappeared, and instead of the family appeared a new polygamy and polyandry, which, in some cases, almost reached promiscuity. It was a terrific social revolution, and yet some traces were retained of the former group life, and the chief remaining institution was the Priest or Medicine-man. He early appeared on the plantation and found his function as the healer of the sick, the interpreter of the Unknown, the comforter of

the sorrowing, the supernatural avenger of wrong, and the one who rudely but picturesquely expressed the longing, disappointment, and resentment of a stolen and oppressed people. Thus, as bard, physician, judge, and priest, within the narrow limits allowed by the slave system, rose the Negro preacher, and under him the first church was not at first by any means Christian nor definitely organized; rather it was an adaptation and mingling of heathen rites among the members of each plantation, and roughly designated as Voodooism. Association with the masters, missionary effort and motives of expediency gave these rites an early veneer of Christianity, and after the lapse of many generations the Negro church became Christian."

—W.E.B. Dubois.

Critics of today's Black church feel that somewhere along the line church leaders have lost their way; that money, or corruption, or a lack of real faith has lured many of them from the principles upon which the church was originally founded.

In far too many Black churches, today, throughout America, Negro preachers, sensing the least lack of cash-flow in the old collection plate will not hesitate to dash like a whirlwind into the pulpit, and scornfully judge certain members of the church for their lack of Christian faith—for their lack of contribution, to the Word—and the Holy Ghost—telling the few males in the congregation that the time has come for them to grow up and become men, and fork over their entire savings to *God Almighty!*—forgetting, that they, too, shall be judged, for being wolves in sheep's clothing; and forgetting that it says somewhere in the Bible, that they, *too*, shall stand before The Judgement Seat.

Is it true, as the above statement seems to suggest, that today's so-called Black pastor is not a help, but a hindrance, not Jesus inspired, but Pharisee driven? Is today's plantation-minded so-called Black preachers really Ol' Massa's greatest ally?

By choosing the safe *hereafter* approach or the *God loves a winner* approach, instead of the more radical let's do for ourselves approach that the early Black church embraced, have sell-out Negro preachers today adopted the old *money* talks and *philosophy* walks, approach?

The Negro Church is particularly culpable for its general lack of concern for the moral and social problems of the community. It has been accommodating. Choosing to focus its attention on heaven and the eternal life, Harold Wingfield writes that the black church was strictly a place in which to engage in the religious experience; it had very little to do with confronting problems of society. Moreover, he asserts that such an orientation caused many to conclude that the black church has an orientation toward black passivity.

—E. U. Essien-Udom, Black Nationalism.

No one was more aware of the Black preachers' lack of concern for this all-important issue, than Martin Luther King, when he said:

"I am sick and tired of seeing Negro preachers riding around in big cars and living in big houses and not concerned about the problems of the people who made it possible for them to get those things... I can hear God saying, Stop preaching your sermons and whooping your irrelevant messes in my face, for your hands are full of tar for the people I have sent you to serve..."

In response to a Black preacher who said that he feared that he would be run out of town if he joined the Movement, King had this say:

"You have three choices: First, you can leave Mississippi, and go to a relatively non-segregated community. Second, you can tacitly accept the Jim Crow laws of Mississippi. Third, you can courageously stand up against them and suffer the consequences."

King was fought tooth and nail by preachers who feared rocking the boat, feared upsetting their private little domains: Throughout the country there were Negro preachers who openly resented King for opening up old wounds, and some, adopting the old FBI line that he was little more than a Communist agitator, denied that he spoke for the greater good of the Black community.

The late Reverend S. M. Wright, in Dallas Texas, who would later have a freeway in the heart of the slums named in his honor (a fitting tribute), refused to meet with King. In Chicago the right Reverend J. H. Jackson, head of the National Baptist Convention and pastor of Olivet Baptist Church, not only called King a hoodlum, and a powder-keg, but upon King's death opposed naming a street in his honor.

The great paradox of the Black preacher has always centered around two conflicting schools of thought. In one corner of the debate are those who think the business of the church is to save souls—providing its members with spiritual guidance that leads to Heaven, while other voices contend that the church should focus more on the downward spiraling lives of their members right here on earth. And this shaky tightrope kind of walk between the worldly and the otherworldly is a walk that very few preachers have mastered to any degree of success. It is a tap dance that can be seen in all Black churches past and present. And the underlying theme is and has always been: The worldly versus the otherworldly, which is *right* and which is *wrong* for the time in which the Black man finds himself.

But King was very forceful on the subject, when he wrote from a jail cell in Birmingham Alabama:

"My dear fellow clergymen… I cannot sit idly by in Atlanta and not be concerned about what happens in Birmingham. Injustice anywhere is a threat to justice everywhere… Actually, we who engage in non-violent direct action are not the creators of tension. We merely bring to the surface the hidden tension that is already alive. We bring it out in the open, where it can be seen and dealt with."

The majority of Black preachers of King's day were fiercely opposed to any movement that threatened their non-existent co-existence with the great White Power Structure; and stayed safely huddled on the sidelines, until the smoke cleared, and their canny instincts told them that it was safe to crawl out of hiding.

C. Eric Lincoln and Lawrence H. Mamiya in their book, The Black Church in the African American Experience surveyed the pastors of 1500 churches, asking the question: Have you been influenced by any of the authors and thinkers of black liberation theology? A mere 35 percent of the Black clergymen who responded answered in the affirmative, while 65 percent said that the liberation of their congregation was no earthly concern of theirs.

Is it any wonder then that the Black Church answered absent when King stood up and read the roll-call for volunteers to step up to the plate? Examining history, the fair observer might easily conclude that *they* were absent then, and *they* have been largely absent ever since.

So absent in fact, that when King openly questioned the blasé leadership of the Black Baptist USA convention, for its passivity on this matter, a fist-fight broke out; one member of the delegation lost three teeth in the pushing and shoving hall-clearing ruckus, while another man died of a heart attack.

The Rev. Anthony Evans, president of the National Black Church Initiative, says, correctly, that: **"A minister, who does not say anything about anybody or cause, and just simply preaches a Gospel that he is not willing to put into action, is a minister not worth having."**

But King not only had to deal with the foot-shuffling foot-dragging dinosaurs within the church, he also found himself at odds with preachers like Reverend Ike; who famously told his congregation to: **"Pledge at least $100! Borrow it! If necessary! People borrow for the doctor and the lawyer, and they save for the undertaker, but rob God! Don't let this be you! Send an extra offering. And be-lieve! For extra blessings!"**

To ease the pain on his poorest members, the gullible grandsons, and granddaughters, of former slaves, the soul-destroying collection plate watching Reverend gave them his blessings, on the installment plan; either by the month, or, by the week.

He reached millions by television and by radio; and was a jagged rock of comfort to his listeners:

"Tell us, sister... Tell us about your original Reverend Ike Prayer Cloth and what it has meant to you!"

"Oh, Reverend Ike! I had me an itch! It was a mean itch, too. I couldn't get rid of it nohow! Then I send away for my Reverend Ike Prayer Cloth and when it arrived in the mail I just swooshed it all over my body... and Reverend..."

"Yes! Yes! Sister! Tell it like it is!"

"The Itch is gone! Reverend Ike. The Itch is gone!"

"Praise God! The sister sent Reverend Ike a Free Will Love Offering; and it is gone! Praise Jesus!"

"It was a mean Itch, too, Reverend Ike!"

"It was a mean itch... and it is gone! Thanks to the Reverend Ike prayer cloth, just like the sister says!"

And not only was the sister's itch gone... but her rent money was also gone, along *with...* the itch.

The community oriented socially conscious Reverend Ike was America's first, Black, prosperity preacher. Born Frederick Joseph Eikerenkoetter the Second, he migrated to Boston in 1964 and founded the Miracle Temple, where he dabbled in faith-healing. Faith healing was a popular craze at that time, "and I was just about the best in Boston, snatching people out of wheelchairs and off their crutches, pouring some oil over them while I commanded them to walk! Or see or hear."

He proudly proclaimed that he was the first Black man in America to preach positive self-image psychology to the black masses within a church setting.

And by preaching positive self-image psychology, he positively bilked his followers out of so much of their hard-earned income, that he could easily afford 16 luxury automobiles.

"My garages runneth over!" he proudly proclaimed to his worshipping idolizing fans.

But in addition to the fleet of luxury cars that were at his beck and call he was also blessed with multi-million dollar mansions and multi-million dollar real estate holdings.

"There was never any doubt about which side Rev. Ike was on when it came to the dispute between Jesus and the money changers in the Temple of Jerusalem. Rev. Ike was always the one yelling that Jesus had no right to shut down his business. He would have argued that God personally told him that turning the Temple into a den of thieves didn't violate any zoning laws. After that incident, he would have gone out of his way to attend Jesus' early morning trial weeks later to make sure his feelings about the anarchist were well known." He would have been the first to shout: "Guilty, guilty!"

—Tony Norman, Pittsburg Post-Gazette.

But the collection-plate-watching socially-conscious-less Reverend Ike, is not the only Negro preacher to shout and stomp and praise the Lord, and fleece the ones they hate out of homes, bank-accounts and the clothes on their backs. There are countless other swindlers, of their ilk. And *now*… a select few of them… shall be called… by name!

Negro Pastor "Sweet Daddy" Grace…!

West Wareham, Massachusetts

Long before Reverend Ike arrived on the scene Sweet Daddy Grace was there taking up the slack, taking, the sons and daughters of former slaves, for all they were worth.

"Salvation is by Grace only! Grace has given God a vacation, and since He is on vacation, don't worry about Him. If you sin against God, Grace can save you, but if you sin against Grace, God cannot save you."
—Sweet Daddy Grace.

Marcelino Manuel da Graca (Sweet Daddy Grace) was born January 25, 1881 or 1884.

In 1926 Grace forked out $39.00 and built a shack that he called a chapel in a place called West Wareham, Massachusetts. And it was there that he founded the United House of Prayer for All People, Church on the Rock of the Apostolic Faith.

Though Grace often preached that "love of money is the root of all evil!" his followers enriched him beyond his wildest dreams.

He had come from Portugal to bring them God, and they would honor him with gifts and call him "Sweet Daddy" —not "Father," but "Daddy"—to acknowledge that he was a loving man who provided and cared for them, unlike the severe ministers of traditional Protestant churches... Critics called him a charlatan, a snake-oil salesman, and a huckster, what with his dozens of opulent abodes, including a Rhine-modeled castle and an 85-room, 21-bathroom mansion in Los Angeles, not to mention his fruit farm in Cuba or his coffee plantation in Brazil. Then there was Grace's claim to be able to perform miracles. But Grace, pointing to himself, would simply retort: "I can only say that if Moses came here now he would have to follow this man."

—A House Divided, Molly Rath.

Bishop Grace claimed that he not only had the power to raise the dead, but that he had actually... raised the dead. A relative traveled the country at his side telling awestruck listeners how he had indeed been raised from the pit of darkness, by the healer, who now had the power of the Holy Ghost.

As his fame spread, so did his wealth.

Chauffer driven high-dollar automobiles, bodyguards, 42 mansions filled with works of art, and income properties throughout the U.S. of A, were just some of the many perks bestowed upon a man who had said that "if Moses came here now, he would follow [me]."

"The old man had some kind of a book that could shake your sickness off, if you put your hands on it. I put my hands on it, and it sure did nearly shake me to pieces. They learned later, the book was made out of electricity. So they ran the old man away from here."
—Callie Washington, former slave, WPA interviewed in the 1930s.

Black church-goers, like the former slave Callie Washington, in far too many places, learn later, that books (and plantation preachers) upon closer examination, aren't always what they appear to be.

"Not everyone who says to me, 'Lord, Lord', will enter the kingdom of heaven, but the one who does the will of my father who is in heaven. On that day many will say to me, 'Lord, Lord, did we not prophesy in your name, and cast out demons in your name, and do many mighty works in your name?' And then will I declare to them, 'I never knew you; depart from me, you workers of lawlessness."

—Matthew 7:21-23.

Negro Pastor Sweet Daddy C. F. Bailey...!

West Wareham, Massachusetts

Bishop Bailey ascended to power on May 23, 2008 when he was elected to head the mammoth United House of Prayer empire (which owns 126 churches in 26 states), during Memorial Week in Washington, D.C.

And on Memorial Day of each year, as though to honor his great Memorial Day victory, and inauguration, Sweet Daddy Baily and his band-led procession parades through the streets of his chosen towns, hoisted on a colorful throne. Pampered by members of his Court, he floats past his well-wishers nodding paternally at the worshipful crowd: a tableau-like picture of invincible royalty.

As he enters his churches his lambs stand in line to shower him with cash: Free-Will love offerings are offered generously to His Holiness as he strolls down the aisles. With great fanfare, the offerings of love are then placed into what the church lovingly refers to as Daddy's Funds, an un-audited, un-searchable account so secretive, that its mysterious far-reaching trail's end ends in a place that is virtually unknowable.

But what is known is that Sweet Daddy lives in a 16,000 square foot gated mansion—one month out of the year. And that he controls real estate, vast amounts of real estate.

As trustee of the United House of Prayer, he landlords over apartments in Washington DC and in his hometown of Charlotte, North Carolina: One of those properties is the McCullough Canaan Land Apartments where a 79-year-old woman made headlines: For her lack of faith in the power of rent money, she was kindly escorted her to her new residence, the curb.

The United House of Prayer along with its head pastor Sweet Daddy Bailey has been accused by their critics of having:

Wrongfully terminating a longtime associate pastor, because he allowed a woman to walk too closely to the 'bishop's mountain' [the pulpit].

Of owning a senior citizen apartment building that evicts elderly tenants.

And:

Accepting tithes from a church member who admits that the money was stolen.

A Washington D.C. woman was religious about her giving to her church, the United House of Prayer for All People… There's just one thing; prosecutors say the money she gave to the church was stolen.

Ephonia Green was sentenced to 46 months in federal prison for embezzling $5.1 million from her job at the non-profit Association of American Medical Colleges. Green admitted doctoring fake invoices with names similar to legitimate institutions like the Brookings Institute to divert the money to herself.

The feds tracked the money to her homes, vacation properties, clothing, cars and her bridal gown business. But there's one other place they say she spent that money, her church, where they say she donated almost $1 million, and was one of the top 10 givers. "The United House of Prayer for All People has more churches in Charlotte than in any other city. Bishop C.M. 'Sweet Daddy' Bailey makes regular visits, as members treat him like royalty. Members shower the Bishop with cash money. He rides in ultra-luxury in a custom-made Maybach automobile from Germany. Bailey lives in mansions owned by the church..."

The United House of Prayer has stood by Ephonia Green, even after the embezzlement charges. This is particularly galling to Rev. Ronald Belton, a Charlotte-based former national evangelist for the church who spent his life in the United House of Prayer.

"She still goes to church, she still has her seat and she's still recognized as top 10," said Belton, who has filed repeated lawsuits after he says the bishop threw him out of the church in a move Belton regards as personal.

I warn everyone who hears the words of the prophecy of this book: if anyone adds to them, God will add to him the plagues described in this book, and if anyone takes away from the words of the book of this prophecy, God will take away his share of the tree of life and in the holy city, which are described in this book.

– Revelation 22:18-19.

Negro Pastor Willard Leonard Jones...!

South Haven, Oklahoma

When the 1921 Tulsa Race riots broke out nearby South Haven became a refuge for Black families fleeing the chaotic burnings and the looting and the wholesale slaughter.

In 1996, when Willard Jones became pastor of a 70-year-old church with only five members, the town that was once a safe harbor for Blacks had fallen upon some mean lean times of its own.

Absentee ownership, property vacancies, and a steep rising increase in crime all added up to one thing for the small country town of South Haven, it needed a savior, and fast.

Willard Jones heard the word; and answered the call.

He had turned a church with five members into a modern bricked establishment with a thriving congregation; now he was ready to tackle an even broader mission: the complete revitalization of the entire community.

"God is love, and you can't confine the love of God to (being inside) church. You've got to take it out to people! People want to see a sermon! Not just hear a sermon! And I believe that is what we're doing here. That [it] is our rule and our charge, to go beyond the walls of the church!"

Jones had had a brainstorm. The thing most lacking in the community was a Community Center. A shelter—as in the old days—for those in need of assistance; a place where free food and free counseling and after-school programs could be gotten for the asking.

"I think we're going to change the mindset [of the community]. People will think somebody cares about them, and they'll want to come in and use these services."

Campaigning tirelessly for donations from corporations, foundations, churches, and individuals alike his brainchild opened its doors in October of 2012.

But as time passed: an audit—of the books—unearthed… troubling news.

Money… was missing.

Huge sums of money: Almost a million dollars.

Someone had stolen $933,507.80!

Someone, had used that stolen money to buy automobiles, and a Rolex watch, and a mink coat, and had bought liquor, and paid for restaurant and casino tabs; someone had devised a scheme that would allow that someone to transfer funds from the Community Center bank account to the Church bank account and into someone's own personal account.

"This case is about a man who abused his position and misappropriated funds belonging to the community center project. Mr. Jones failed to honor the trust of the community." —U.S. Attorney Danny Williams.

In January of 2015, Willard Leonard Jones, the savior who had said that God is love and you can't confine the love of God to the church, was sentenced to 37 months in prison, and was ordered to pay restitution in the amount of $933,507.80.

Beware of false prophets, who come to you in sheep's clothing but inwardly are ravenous wolves.

—Matthew 7:15

Negro Pastor Abraham Kennard...

Rome, Georgia

Pastor Kennard, who had served time for armed robbery, had a plan: A plan to raise money for his fellow pastors. For a three-thousand-dollar investment, $500,000 would bless the pastors' collection plates—in short order—and it would be like manna from Heaven.

And for every new pastor a pastor brought into the fold that pastor would receive an additional $500 signing bonus!

Within a year, Kennard had signed checks totaling hundreds of thousands of dollars, to new recruits, and all seemed to be going precisely as planned.

Rural, impoverished black churches were reaping the benefits of a plan that could not fail.

At check-signing events with praise music blaring in the background Kennard would prance to and fro across the pulpit shouting halleluiahs, for as he had promised, small black churches throughout the country were reaping the blessings of the faith-offerings that he had cast upon the waters of glory.

Kennard had promised a number of churches that they would see a return of as much as three million dollars for their investments.

And it seemed as if God was smiling from Heaven.

But then, suddenly… the halleluiahs from the pulpit turned sour, cold, and silent.

Some churches had not received a payment in six, seven, eight, or nine months; and pastors across the country were beginning to… ask questions: Where is the money…? Where is that great blessing that they were promised?

The blessing, it turned out, had been bestowed on Kennard's lavish lifestyle: on his luxury cars, on his mansion, and on his expensive clothes and jewelry.

When suspicious preaches who hadn't been paid in months began to make waves, Kennard went on the offensive, urging them to keep it cool because the checks were definitely in the mail.

But in June of 2002 when the heat around his ankles ignited into a bonfire, he gathered his fellow pastors at a meeting in Orlando Florida… And dropped an atomic bombshell: When he announced that the preachers who had invested in his scam would not be paid, the enraged audience stood up in protest, many of them heading for the doors.

"How many of you are judging me right now!" Kennard shouted at their backs, wounded, to the core, by their lack of faith. "If you are judging me, you are judging God!"

In July of that year, disgruntled ministers called in the FBI to investigate what to them was beginning to look more and more like a Ponzi scheme. The FBI judged that they might be correct. Then in January of 2003 the Bureau raided Kennard's estate, seizing boxes of bank statements, and business records: They discovered that it would have cost Kennard nine billion dollars to honor the contracts he had signed with the ministers he had duped. He had swindled 1600 churches out of more than nine million dollars.

At his trial in 2004 Kennard claimed the Government was trying to hang him on a cross. For he had intended to repay every dime of the money he had taken from his fellow ministers, but the Government had barged in as he had sat down to write the check.

On February 7, 2005 he was convicted on 116 counts and received 17 years in prison. The Prophet, the Disciple, who had come like Abraham in the Bible, has gone to his reward in prison.

But false prophets also arose among the people, just as there will be false teachers among you, who will secretly bring in destructive heresies, even denying the Maker who brought them, bringing upon themselves swift destruction.

—2 Peter 2:1.

Negro Pastor Henry (the Deacon) Lyons...!
Pinellas County, Florida

Conceived by a father he despised, Henry Lyons was born January 17, 1942, in Gainesville Florida. His father had told him that he had been conceived in a ditch; and then showed him the ditch. And Lyons, by all accounts, never forgave the old man for the act, or, for having confessed the act, or, for showing him the place where the act occurred.

Lyons was elected president of the National Baptist Convention USA Inc. in 1994. Reverend J. H. Jackson (who had called Martin Luther King a hoodlum and a powder-keg) had helped to engineer his own defeat by welcoming Lyons into the NBC as an assistant to the General Secretary of the world's second largest Baptist denomination in the United States. Jackson who had ruled the NBC with an iron hand since 1953 was soon dethroned, and Lyons found himself at the helm of an organization that had over 10 million members.

In his position as president of the NBC he had direct access to the White House when Clinton was President. Hillary Clinton sat erect and proudly at one of his services at St. Petersburg Bethel Baptist Church, his headquarters and residency.

Lyons had assumed leadership of the NBC promising to save the organization from the excesses of the previous administration.

But in April of 1996, Lyon stood teary-eyed before Judge Susan Schaeffer, repentant, and sorry, for his crimes:

"I plead for mercy," he cried; but none was given.

He was sentenced to 5 ½ years in prison for swindling more than four million dollars from the National Baptists Convention USA.

He had also been convicted the previous month for bilking companies that wanted to sell cemetery products, life insurance policies and credit cards to members of the NBC, and, for stealing money donated to rebuild burned Southern black churches. It had also been reported that he had stolen $50,000 that had come from the National Coalition on Black Voter Participation Inc., a noble cause that was created to increase Black turnout on election days.

While the prosecuting U.S. Attorney believes that Lyons should be held accountable for his actions, members of his flock do not: he is now the pastor of a church in Tampa Florida.

A victim: of the white man's oppression.

...If anyone aspires to the office of overseer, he desires a noble task. Therefore an overseer must be above reproach, the husband of one wife, sober-minded, self-controlled, respectable, hospitable, able to teach, not a drunkard, not violent but gentle, not quarrelsome, not a lover of money. He must manage his own household well, with all dignity keeping his children submissive, for if someone does not know how to manage his own household, how will he care for God's church?

—1 Timothy 3:1-16.

Arlington, Texas

Terry Hornbuckle, a minister, a comforter, to his flock, was accused and convicted by a Texas court: for raping members of his own congregation.

Hornbuckle lured Krystal to a Euless apartment in the summer of 2003 with the promise of a birthday present. He gave her $120. He also drugged and raped her. Before that night, she told the court, she was a virgin. Why did she accompany him in the first place? Her plaintive answer: "He was my bishop."

—Inside the Terry Hornbuckle Case, Andrea Grimes and Stephanie Morris, Dallas Observer.

In 1986 Hornbuckle had founded Victory Temple Bible Church in Arlington, Texas, with only fifteen members occupying the mostly empty pews. In 1999 the 15-member church had mushroomed into a lavish 30,000 square foot mega church, and was growing.

The bishop encouraged their ambitions and cultivated their attentions. He would sometimes call up groups of single moms and bathe them in compliments and words of encouragement. He probably didn't fail to notice that many of them were beautiful, vulnerable and looking for a man to provide love and stability in their lives.

In recent years, the calls for offerings reportedly intensified... On Sundays, Hornbuckle would often ask everyone who hadn't given their tithe—a donation of 10 percent of one's income, a common practice in Pentecostal churches—to raise their hands. Many were embarrassed but took it as inspiration to work harder and give more to their bishop. Pay your rent last, he said, and give Agape your tithe, the "first fruits." God will provide.

Gradually he became a figurehead in the black church world. Bishop T.D. Jakes wrote a laudatory blurb for one of Hornbuckle's self-published books. The bishop hung out with Michael Irvin and Deion Sanders; he'd brag from the pulpit. He knew Quincy Carter. Emmitt Smith even wrote a letter to Tarrant County prosecutors extolling the virtues of Hornbuckle and his marriage to Renee. The couple had counseled Smith and his wife, he wrote, and he looked up to them. In his eyes, they had the perfect marriage.

And there were a lot of good things going on at Agape under the Hornbuckles. Church leaders helped people buy homes and build better job skills. Maybe they could live in a $742,000 house, just like the Hornbuckles. He'd tell them how they could save up and drive expensive cars, such as his Cadillac Escalade. All blessings from God... But behind the bishop was the man. A man addicted to women, power and, in the end, drugs. It would ultimately cost him his church and his freedom.

—Inside the Terry Hornbuckle Case, Andrea Grimes and Stephanie Morris, Dallas Observer.

At his trial, one of his victims claimed that he had had sex with her in the back of a church van.

A married member of the church described an intimate rather bizarre sexual encounter with the defendant, which caused her severe abdominal pains.

Another testified that Hornbuckle had tried to seduce her while her husband was undergoing rehab therapy for alcohol addiction.

Just before 5 p.m., Judge Wisch read the sentences slowly and deliberately. Fourteen years for the sexual assault of Krystal Buchanan; 10 years for the sexual assault of "Jane Doe"; 15 years for the sexual assault of "Kate Jones."

Hornbuckle will serve his sentence terms concurrently, potentially putting the bishop behind bars for the next 15 years, though he will be eligible for parole after serving half that time. The jury fined Hornbuckle a total of $30,000—the maximum allowed— for the three criminal cases.

After years of preaching prosperity, assuring his congregation that they could achieve material wealth through faithful giving, Terry Hornbuckle is now broke... {Compounding his troubles} the bishop also has the civil lawsuit pending against him, and if he loses

that, he may owe millions more to the other women who claim he raped them.

—Inside the Terry Hornbuckle Case, Andrea Grimes and Stephanie Morris, Dallas Observer.

Everyone who goes on ahead and does not abide in the teachings of Christ does not have God. Whoever abides in the teachings has both the Father and the Son. If anyone comes to you and does not bring this teaching, do not receive him into your house or give him any greeting, for whoever greets him takes part in his wicked works.

—2 John 1:9-11

Negro Pastor Craig Lamar Davis...!

Atlanta, Georgia

Two women, who didn't know the other existed, went to the Atlanta Georgia Police with a weird, almost unbelievable story:

A pastor at a local church had given them the HIV virus—knowingly—and that he considered himself to be a real lady-killer.

Literally.

Two women are accusing married Atlanta pastor Craig Lamar Davis of Full Gospel Baptist Church of spreading HIV, IB Times reports. The women said they had affairs with Davis but that he did not tell them he is HIV positive.

Davis was arrested July 22 on charges of reckless conduct and was released from Fulton County Jail two days later on $1,500 bond.

Ronita McAfee said she started talking to Davis on Facebook, and the two began having an affair. He never informed her of his HIV positive status, but called McAfee a couple of months after the affair started and told her one of his ex-girlfriends had tested positive for HIV. He told McAfee to get tested but that it wasn't a death sentence if the test came back positive. McAfee tested negative but that hasn't stopped her from trying to warn other women about Davis. In an email sent to BlackMediaScoop.com, she said:

"Mr. Craig Lamar Davis is a master manipulator: women have bought him cars, relocated and purchased homes under the impression that he was going to marry them, bought him countless suits and accessories (i.e. watches, ties, jewelry, shoes, etc.), given him their food stamp cards every month as if he's entitled, depleted their checking and savings account on his behalf, etc. and he expects nothing less."

McAfee also said that Davis shows "no regard for the human life" and that she was just wanted to let the people of the church know that he has been "sexually rampant."

One of his victims had been abstinent for 15 years. When she went to her doctor for a yearly checkup she was stunned, when her doctor told her that she had the HIV virus.

The second woman involved in the case was told to chill, because: "With HIV, you can still live, it's not the end of the world."

When she asked him why he hadn't told her about his deadly disease before sleeping with her, he said, God had spoken to him: and had told him to, keep still.

Lay not up for yourselves treasures upon earth, where moth and rust doth corrupt, and where thieves break through and steal: But lay up for yourselves treasures in heaven, where neither moth nor rust doth corrupt, and where thieves do not break through nor steal: For where your treasure is, there will your heart be also. — Matthew 6:19-21... **If any man will come after me, let him deny himself, and take up his cross, and follow me.**

—Matthew 16:24.

Plantation Negro preachers, did we hear you say, Amen! To that?

Chapter Eight
Plantation Negro Politicians

In 1967 Carl Stokes was elected as the first Black mayor of a major American city.

His election had given the Black race collectively a big sigh of relief. Thank God a 'mighty! At long last! A Black man was given the chance to wield the whip of power, and at last, at lon-n-g last! The Black race would take its place under the sun!

But high-flying rhetoric is one thing reality another?

Because as other Black mayors and black officials began to pop up all across the country, from the '70s on into the '80s and '90s, still, there was no noticeable change in the overall wealth of the Black community. In fact, in some cities where Black mayors and Black city councilmen had reined for years conditions steadily got worse.

Cointelpro—J. Edgar Hoover's Frankenstein Monster—had been designed to infiltrate, co-opt, or destroy the Civil Rights Movement by whatever means necessary. But if the Movement could not be killed off, entirely, if remnants of that struggle had been subdued, but were still struggling in the throes of death, then, could what was left of the Struggle… be bought off?

Could there be… Black… co-conspirators… who throughout history has worked hand in hand, with Ol Massa—behind the scenes?

Black co-conspirators from slavery to this day, have gleefully helped Ol Massa catch people they don't like, old, and young alike. This especially holds true for Negro politicians.

Uncle Simon was a kind of overseer. Whenever he told his master the slaves did something wrong, the slaves were whipped, and Uncle Simon was whipped too. I asked him why he should be whipped, he hadn't done anything wrong. But Uncle Simon said he guessed he needed it anyway.

    —Julia King, former slave, interviewed in the 1930s by the WPA.

And so, the question is this:

When the Civil Rights Movement was all but destroyed, in the '70s, '80s and '90s, had Black politicians of that era turned their backs on Dr. King's drum major battle cry, to take up the battle cry of old Uncle Simon? Uncle Simon knew that he would get the same whipping that his fellow slaves got, but unable to help himself, unable to go against the grain of his nature, he simply submitted himself to the whipping that he thought he *needed* anyway.

An outbreak of scandals within the Black political establishment then and now has to make one wonder: if in fact, Black elected officials were, and are today, working in league with Uncle Simon's ghostly old memory.

In most cities [where there are black Mayors or Black representatives] you have politically, criminally incompetent Blacks in office... There are members in the Black Caucus who will not stick up for Black folks. They're so busy taking care of everybody except the Black folk who put them into office. They don't have sense enough to know that as soon as those parties that they are supporting gets strong enough, they are going to take them out of office... Black folks don't get anything when Black politicians are

out of office, and they don't get anything when Black politicians are in office.

—Dr. Claud Anderson, former assistant Secretary of Commerce.

Malcolm X said that it is not necessary to change the white man's mind. "We have to change our own mind! You can't change *his* mind about us. We've got to change *our* minds about each other. We have to see each other with new eyes. We have to see each other as brothers and sisters. We have to come together with warmth so we can develop unity and harmony that's necessary to get this problem solved for ourselves."

But were the words of Malcolm X lost on future Black politicians? Many have strayed, and gone to prison. And almost all of them have abandoned the march that those old-time slaves set out upon in 1865.

Today's Black politicians seem to have learned a basis lesson of politics: You dance with the one who brought you to the party. And they appear to have learned through bitter experience that one can serve only one master at a time. One can serve the ones who *voted* for him, or serve the ones who *financed* him.

A dilemma faced by all politicians, but more acutely by Black politicians, who in many cases come into office lacking wealth or wealthy donors who are interested in Black affairs. But by serving the interest of his white financiers, Black politicians becomes a sort of Negro Uncle Simon; a puppet dancing to the tune of his handler behind the curtains, because he thinks he deserves to be punished.

To the jaded eye the game of *plantation politics* appears to function, very successfully, in the following fashion:

The Black do-nothing politician knowing that he can get nothing done in a rigged political system deflects his own do-nothingness onto the hated do-nothingness of his white thoroughly disgusting political enemy; his best friend.

Concealing the fact that he and his hated enemy both receive their marching orders from the same rich white campaign donors, the Negro politician appears to have mastered the art of do-nothing politics to such an extent, that he is able to get elected time and time again, by those that he does nothing for, time and time again.

The Rouge's Gallery of Negro Uncle Simon Politicians

The Negro politicians who live in infamy, the ones who take a whipping from their Ol' Massa, because they think they deserve it, you scoundrels, shall now, be called, *by* name…

Negro Politician Ray Nagin…!

New Orleans, Louisiana

Best remembered as the Mayor of New Orleans when Hurricane Katrina flooded almost 80 percent of the city, Nagin had promised the citizens of New Orleans a government that was free of corruption, a government that would revitalize the city's failed outdated economy.

In 1998, the local alternative newspaper Gambit Weekly named Nagin its New Orleanian of the Year. Announcing his candidacy for Mayor in 2001, he said: "The city needs a different type of leader, someone who had business acumen," and he said that he was compelled to enter the race after talking to his son and his son's friends: "They told me they didn't see a future for themselves in New Orleans," he confided to Autumn C. Giusti of the New Orleans Magazine.

But many long-time residents were skeptical.

The city has a long sordid history of corruption; and those in the know knew that the wheels of City Hall were greased with bribes, and that close, personal connections with corrupt, unsavory characters, was a ritualistic realistic common practice.

Handily defeating his police chief opponent in a run-off election Nagin told his elated followers that he had *challenged* his inner circle to think outside the box, "as new thinkers, as change agents, as a group trying to make the city better!"

And on the surface, he seemed to practice what he preached: Two months into his term he had ordered the arrest of 84 people on corruption charges, one of his relatives among the group. "We are in a battle for the soul of New Orleans!" he proclaimed… "The perception that you have to do business under the table, whether it's real or imagined, if you want to do business in New Orleans is fading!"

Two days before the arrival of Hurricane Katrina Nagin warned New Orleans residents to board up their homes and evacuate.

But the evacuation was not mandatory.

And on Monday the 29 of 2005, the storm roared into the city, the levees around the city exploded; and 80 percent of the city was now filled like a giant bowl of water.

And Americans were horrified when the federal government sat on its rump for five long death-dealing days before rendering a response to one of the deadliest disasters in American history.

Nagin, the Defender of the City, became a household name. But his detractors accused him of dragging his feet. He should have moved more forcefully to evacuate the poor out of the city, his critics charged. And television footage of dozens of buses submerged in water that could have been used to evacuate the poor to safe ground, appeared to back up their claims.

Quick to deflect his negligence onto others, he declared that Hurricane Katrina was a sign that "God is mad at America" over the war in Iraq and over African Americans committing violence against each other!

But behind the scenes Nagin had begun to fall into the same trap his predecessors had fallen into.

And those in the know were not surprised when powerful insiders wormed their way into his inner circle.

And suddenly a career that had started out on a high note, a career built on the notion that City Hall belonged to the *people*, was now embroiled in the same kind of bribes and kickbacks scandals that his predecessors had found themselves embroiled in going back decades. And in the end 20 counts of felonious crimes were laid at his feet:

At his trial, he never once showed an ounce of repentance or remorse, never admitted guilt of any kind. Relying on the same, tired old, blame everyone except the innocent one before you, defense, he piously proclaimed, "I trust God is going to work all this out."

Prosecutors claimed that he had lied 22 times on the witness stand.

And Assistant U.S. Attorney Matthew Coman was not convinced by his testimony or by his claims of innocence.

"These repeated violations, at the expense of the citizens of New Orleans in a time when honest leadership was needed most, do not deserve leniency." And none was given. Nagan received ten years for his crimes against the gullible great, great, grandsons and granddaughters of former slaves; who had placed their dreams in the hands of common, corruptible man.

I think slavery was a mighty good thing for mother, father, me and the other members of the family, and I cannot say anything but good for my old master and missus... For myself and them, I will say again, slavery was a mighty good thing.

—Mary Anderson, former slave, WPA interviewed in the 1930s.

There were a few well-treated slaves, who thought that slavery was a good thing; they were never beaten by their masters, and as long as they behaved themselves, they weren't sold, or mistreated.

Today there are some Black politicians, who believe that modern day slavery is a good thing. Their white political benefactors treat them kindly; they eat well, they aren't singled out for the abuse that their field-hand constituents get; and as long as they toe the line, tap-dancing and monkey shining for Massa, they can become rich, and famous, on the backs of the ones picking the cotton.

Negro Politician Kwame Kilpatrick…!

Detroit, Michigan

Elected to the Michigan House of Representatives in 1996, Kilpatrick was elevated to minority floor leader for the Michigan Democratic Party in 1998, and served in that capacity until the year 2000. He became the youngest mayor in the history of Detroit at the age of 31 in the year 2002. In his inaugural address, he stood before an enthusiastic crowd of Black well-wishers and shouted:

"I *stand* before you as a son of the city of Detroit, and all that it represents! I was *born* here in the city of Detroit, I was raised here in the city of Detroit, I went to these Detroit Public Schools and I understand this city… This position is personal to me. It's much more than just politics."

But the echoes of his famous "I am a son of Detroit" speech was still ringing piously in the air when in the same year it was alleged that Kilpatrick had thrown a wild out-of-control party at his Manoogian Mansion, the city owned residence of the mayor.

The mayor's police security team later filed a report with Internal Affairs claiming that the mayor's wife Carlita had attacked a female stripper at the party.

Officer Harold C. Nelthrope and Internal Affairs Officer Gary Brown later alleged that they were fired for investigating the mayor's unsavory conduct, and under a Whistleblower's lawsuit were awarded an 8.4-million-dollar settlement.

The following year in 2003, Tamara Green, the stripper who allegedly had been attacked by Carlita Kilpatrick at the Mayor's residence, was murdered.

Shot dead by a .40 caliber Glock pistol, the type used by the Detroit police department. And some members of the Police department believed that her murder was a hit by members within their *own* department. Another officer also alleged that his investigation into the stripper's murder precipitated his removal from the case, and his transfer out of the Homicide Division. The officer also alleged that his superiors within the department went out of their way to sabotage his investigation into the murdered Tamara Green, whose telephone number linked her to other high-ranking officials within the Kilpatrick administration.

But the case on the murdered stripper went cold. Very suddenly.

But in 2007, "The Son of Detroit" was in hot water again, on trial, along with his chief of staff, Christine Beatty, for denying that they were involved in a hot extramarital affair.

And Kilpatrick was *outraged.*

"My mother is a congresswoman! There have always been strong women around me! My aunt is a state legislator! I find it's absurd to assert that every woman that works with a man is a whore! I think it's disrespectful! Not just to Christine Beatty, but to women who do a professional job that they do every single day! And it's disrespectful for their families as well!"

But text messages between the mayor and his married chief of staff proved beyond a shadow of doubt that they really were involved in a sexual relationship. Text messages also proved that the Mayor and Mrs. Beatty (who became famous for telling a cop who had ticketed her for speeding, "Do you know who the f—I am!) used city funds for their midnight rendezvous, and that they conspired to fire a police officer for investigating the murder of Tamara Green."

And Kilpatrick using race as his defense was outraged. Again.

"There's race in this! And we run from it in this region! And I think it's impossible for us to move forward as a region without confronting it head-on!"

In 2007, WXYZ TV reported that Kilpatrick channeled $8,600 from the Kilpatrick Civic Fund to take his wife, three sons, and babysitter, for a week-long vacation to a five-star California resort. The fund had been created to improve voter education, crime prevention, and economic empowerment for his faithful supporters. And Kilpatrick was outraged, outraged, as he grabbed the microphone from the hand of a TV reporter, and tossed it aside.

In 2008 the Detroit City Council pleaded with Kilpatrick to resign from office. The vote was seven to one in favor of the request.

The non-binding resolution asking the good Mayor to resign had cited 33 reasons for him to resign, but The Son of Detroit was outraged. Again. Resign? Never!

Shortly afterwards, Wayne County Prosecutor Kym Worthy handed down a 12-count criminal indictment against "The Son of Detroit" and his chief of staff, Christine Beatty. Kilpatrick was charged with eight felonies. Beatty was charged with seven felonies, and both were charged with perjury, obstruction of justice, and misconduct in office.

In autumn of 2008 Michigan Attorney General Mike Cox filed two felony charges against Kilpatrick for assaulting or interfering with a law officer. Kilpatrick was alleged to have shoved a police officer who was attempting to serve a subpoena on a friend of the mayor's.

Shortly afterwards Kilpatrick pled guilty to two felony counts of obstruction of justice, and no contest to assaulting the police officer who was attempting to serve the subpoena to his friend. He consented to serve four months in jail, surrender his license to practice law, and to pay one million dollars of restitution to the city of Detroit. He also agreed to five years of probation and to stay out of politics during the period of his probation. He agreed to resign as mayor and surrender his pension from the Michigan House of Representatives. And he later admitted that he had lied under oath on several occasions.

In December of 2009 another bombshell: it was revealed in a court hearing that Kilpatrick had received undocumented loans from several prominent Detroit businessmen amounting to approximately $240,000.00.

In June of 2010, the Detroit News reported that Kilpatrick's father, Bernard, and the Kilpatrick Civic Fund, may have played a significant role in a sludge-hauling contract awarded to Synagro Technologies Incorporated. Synagro had contributed generously to Kilpatrick Civic Fund. The Tech Company had also provided Kilpatrick with free airplane trips to Mackinac Island and to Las Vegas, Nevada. No charges were filed against Mayor Kilpatrick in this case, but Rayford Jackson, a Synagro consultant, was later convicted of bribery in the case.

In the same month and year, the Mayor was indicted on 19 federal counts of criminality, among them 10 counts of mail fraud, three counts of wire fraud, one count of tax evasion, and five counts of filing a false tax return.

It was also alleged that Kilpatrick as a Michigan Legislator had funneled state grant money to U.N.I.T.E. a company owned by his wife Carlita. It was also alleged that he had devised a scheme to use Kilpatrick Civic Fund to finance his mayoral campaign, and to cover expenses incurred for golf clubs, summer camp for his children, a lease on a Cadillac Deville, personal travel, moving expenses, and various focus groups.

The Detroit Free Press examining city records found that 29 of Kilpatrick's friends and family members had been appointed to positions in various city departments. The mayor had eliminated thousands of city jobs but had found positions for friends and cronies who had little or no experience in performing the work assigned to them.

In 2012 another bombshell: the Securities and Exchange Commission indicted The Son of Detroit and former city treasurer Jeffrey W. Beasley for receiving $125,000.00 worth of travel and other perks from Mayfield Gentry Realty Advisors.

Finally: on March 11th, 2013, Kwame Kilpatrick's job as a one-man demolition crew, ended, when he was found guilty on 24 counts of bribery, racketeering, extortion, and fraud, and was sentenced to serve 28 years in prison. With time off for good behavior, his earliest possible release date was set to be August 1, 2037.

Judge Nancy Edmunds, the presiding judge, said, as she handed down the verdict: **"It is necessary to examine the defendant's history as a whole, pointing to the money that was supposed to go toward city necessities and instead, was given to friends and family… One thing is certain. It was the citizens of Detroit who suffered."**

As so often happens in cases like this, the religious community, Kilpatrick's fiercest most loyal supporters (totally ignoring the fact that their *friend* the Mayor had swindled them out of millions of dollars, had transferred $500,000.00 from funds for children and senior services to a close friend) gathered outside the courtroom after the trail with cries of unfair treatment of black public officials, with cries of racism, with cries of how the good mayor was one of them, and would remain one of *them*.

"You asks me what I thinks of Massa Lincoln? Well, I thinks that he was doin' the worst thing that he could to turn all them fool niggers loose."

—Henry Bobbitt, former slave, WPA interviewed in the 1930s.

Today's Negro politicians, like the old former slave Henry Bobbitt, thinks that Massa Lincoln should not have turned all them fool niggers loose in the first place.

Negro Politician Sharpe James...!

Newark, New Jersey

Newark New Jersey mayor from 1986 to 2006, Sharpe James had come into office promising the city a *renaissance*. Driving a Rolls Royce, and piloting his own yacht, he professed to be for the *common man* on the streets.

His opponent in 2002 was Cory Booker, a thirty-two-year-old Black lawyer and community activist, who had set up his campaign headquarters in the crime-infested Brick Towers housing projects.

In one of the most heated campaigns the city had ever experienced James launched a savage attack against his young political rival, accusing him of accepting donations from the Ku Klux Klan, of being a faggot white boy, and alleging that Booker was secretly Jewish and was working hand in hand with the white establishment to sabotage the Black community. He was not 'black enough' to lead. "You have to *learn* to be an African American, and we don't have time to *train* you!"

So intense was the battle for the mayor's job that a PBS documentary entitled, Street Fight, was produced showing how Booker's supporters had been trailed by the police, how Cory Booker's phone had been tapped, and how he had been police escorted out of city parks and public housing projects. Tenants in those housing projects had been warned by public housing authorities that they could be evicted if they displayed Booker signs in their windows.

And making matters worse for Booker, was the fact that the entrenched, entire Black power structure had thrown its very formidable weight against the young upstart, and stood staunchly in support of their established establishment cohort.

Booker lost the election.

But in July of 2007 the mayor who had said that Cory Booker was not 'black enough' to serve the Black community, was charged in a thirty-three-count indictment that included charging $58,000 in personal expenses to a municipal credit card. He was also charged with rigging the sale of public real estate for the benefit of his young trophy mistress, Tamika Riley, who then resold the properties, netting five hundred thousand dollars in profit.

On April 16, 2008 the Renaissance Man, the only man in the 2002 race for mayor who was 'black enough' to serve the Black community, was sentenced to two years in prison, for *sticking it* to the Black community; that he loved.

One time there, some white mens comes down the river on a boat and they comes into the fields and talks to a gang of us and they says that our masters ain't treatin' us right. They tells us that we [should] be paid for our work… I laughs at 'em, but some of them fool niggers listens to 'em… I goes and tells the marster… He says to me, I wants you to help me. I says, 'Yas sar, marster'. I does like he tells me to do. And that night the niggers marches in [the storehouse] and sneaks their guns in too. I is lyin' up in the loft… I gits out of the window and I runs to the house and tells the marster. Then me

an' him and the young marster goes out and I slams the pack house door and I locks it… The niggers "liberates for a few minutes and then they throws the guns out. I knows how many they has got so I counts till they throw them all out, then I gathers up them guns and I totes 'em off to the big house… Well suh, we keeps them niggers shet up fer about a week on short rations; and at the end of that time them niggers is cured for good."

—Uncle David Blount, former slave, WPA narrative.

Uncle Blount, who *knew* his place on the old plantation, appears to have become the perfect role model—for the plantation-minded, modern day, Negro politician?

Negro Politician Tony Mack…!

Trenton, New Jersey

"Nearly four years ago, Tony Mack raised his hand and swore to uphold the state and federal constitutions as he assumed the office of mayor of the capital city of New Jersey," U.S. Attorney Fishman said, when Tony Mack was sentenced to 58 months in prison. "[But] within 10 weeks, he began selling that office and, with the help of his brother and others, he sold out the people of Trenton in the process. Today, he learned the true cost of his actions: He will spend 58 months in federal prison."—United States Attorney's Office, New Jersey.

Tony Mack was elected mayor of Trenton New Jersey in 2010. And almost immediately, when the polls closed signaling the end of the race, more than 300 of his campaign workers showed up at a local donut shop demanding payment for their services, complaining that they had not been paid as promised: "My term will not start with people who supported me being angry about not being paid," they were told. "It will be taken care of! I will do right by them."

But a year later in 2011 he would face a recall election. Angry residents who signed the petition questioned the lack of experience of the city department heads who had replaced those that had been fired who had worked for the previous administration. Others complained about the mayor's handling of a recent flood that had forced them out of their homes.

"He didn't come down here right away," said one angry resident, "and when he *did* all he wanted to do was put his arm around you and take a picture."

Claiming he had done the best that he could do given the city's dire financial straits he said that most of the people spearheading the recall effort had an axe to grind, politically.

"If you analyze those that are part of the recall, and you factor in their requests to me, then it'll be crystal clear as to why they're doing what they're doing. Most of them have come to me for either a contract or a job."

The recall fell short by more than 2,000 signatures, but the following year on September 10, 2012 Mack was arrested on bribery, fraud, extortion and money laundering charges. He was removed from office in 2014, and was later sentenced to serve time in prison, for his crimes against the ones he scorned.

Mack who had promised to protect the interest of the Black citizens of Trenton New Jersey had turned out to be just another race-selling Negro politician; who was only interested… in his *own* interests.

We wasn't happy at the surrender and we cussed ole Abraham Lincoln all over the place. We was told the disadvantages of not havin' no education, but shucks, we don't need no book learnin' with ole marster to look after us.

—John Beckwith, former slave, WPA interviewed in the 1930s.

Who needs book learning—when Negro politicians are on the job, 24/7—to look after… *us*…?

Negro Politician Clarence Norman...!

New York City, New York

In October of 2002 a nurse called the hotline of the District Attorney's office. She was in a child custody dispute with her husband. She suspected that her husband had bribed the judge who had been assigned to handle her case. The District Attorney had her wired and after a secret meeting with the *fixer* who had arranged the Bribe the judge was wiretapped and, in return for a lenient sentence, implicated one of the most powerful political operatives in New York City: New York alderman Clarence Norman.

Clarence Norman, Jr. is the son of Clarence Norman, the politically influential head pastor of the First Baptist Church of Crown Heights. He came to power promising what most Negro politicians promise: Change.

But there seemed to be something, fishy, in New York, from the moment he took office.

And it didn't take a *nose scientist* to figure out the direction in which that fishy odor was coming from: City Hall.

When the corrupt judge saw the evidence the DA had gathered concerning his corrupt activities on the bench, he, too, consented to be wired, and in short order fingers began to point at the change-maker himself.

"Clarence Norman Jr., the deposed Democratic assemblyman and party leader from Brooklyn, was convicted yesterday of extortion in what prosecutors said was a scheme to shake down judicial candidates in exchange for party support. It was his third conviction on corruption charges in 17 months.

In a split verdict, a jury in State Supreme Court in Brooklyn convicted him of coercion, grand larceny by extortion and attempted grand larceny by extortion, while acquitting him of five similar counts.

Prosecutors said Mr. Norman had coerced two candidates for civil court judge to pay thousands of dollars to favored campaign consultants, or lose his organization's support in the 2002 primary."

—Anemona Hortocollis, New York Times.

Norman, a powerbroker who empowered himself was sentenced to three to nine years behind bars on charges of grand larceny, and falsifying business records.

Dem wuz good days, Boss Man. I sho wish I could call them [slave] times back again. The old marsters and the young marsters, they jes knock about over the country on their hosses, and the young misses and the old misses, they ride about in the fine carriages with the coachman doin' the drivin'. The marsters and the misses, they look after their niggers good.

—Henry Green, former slave, WPA interview in the 1930s.

The marsters and the misses looked after the niggers good, then, and are looking after the niggers, good, now.

Thanks to their lap-sitting pinkie-waving yassuh bossing Negro politician pals, they are looking after the niggers, really, *really*, good.

Negro Politician Michael McGee…!

Milwaukee, Wisconsin

Michael McGee Jr. was elected city alderman of Milwaukee Wisconsin in April of 2004.

And good news turned to bad news on McGee's very first day in office. On the day that he was elected, the principle at a local school complained to University of Wisconsin officials that McGee had tried to persuade students to skip class and campaign to get him elected instead. He would later apologize for acting… inappropriately.

In November of the following year, he was cited for resisting arrest, disorderly conduct and was placed under arrest. He pled no contest to resisting and obstructing an officer in the performance of his duty and in turn the city dropped the disorderly conduct beef.

And if things had gotten off to a bad start for the young popular former wrestling star, the worst was yet to come.

Whispers of malfeasance, and corruption, were heard from various business owners in McGee's district: The FBI was called in to investigate. A sting operation unearthed evidence that McGee was shaking down local businesses—demanding bribes for liquor licenses. His mistake: the one that landed him in jail? Was the mistake he made in attempting to shake down a patsy; who moonlighted, as an undercover FBI agent.

But a secret wiretap had unearthed something far more sinister: a plot to do bodily harm (murder) to a man, who had burglarized the home of a friend. The FBI took the threats serious enough to shut down the investigation and arrest McGee on charges that included conspiracy to commit murder, and conspiracy to commit substantial battery—on the body parts—of a human being.

His down spiraling career would come to a sudden fiery crash on June 24 of 2008, when a jury, after six hours of deliberation, would find him guilty of having committed nine (known) felonies, and he was sentenced to six- and one-half years behind bars.

Yes sir, Boss Man… it would be a heap better for it to be like it was then, because we never had nothing' to worry about: except to do what we was told to do… Our marster trained us up right, for to do our work good, and to obey what the white folks say and to be polite to the white folks; and after we left old marster then our mother she trained us the same way.

—Henry Green, former slave, WPA interview in the 1930s.

Negro politicians have been trained the same way—for years.

Negro Politician Patrick Cannon...!

Charlotte, North Carolina

On November 5, 2013, Patrick Cannon was elected mayor of Charlotte, North Carolina. Weeks before the election, he had this to say:

"The one thing you have to have in an elected official is somebody who will *not* be subservient to *anybody*... I let people know up front that [giving money] doesn't guarantee you anything in the terms of a vote from Patrick Cannon."

Less than a year later, he had this to say:

I hereby give notice of my resignation from the position of the Mayor of the City of Charlotte, effective immediately... In light of the charges that have been brought against me, it is my judgment that the pendency of these charges will create too much of a distraction for the business of the City to go forward smoothly and without interruption.

Cannon had been accused of accepting bribes from undercover FBI agents on five different occasions. On one of those occasions, he had taken the bills and fanned them near his ear, with approval. On another occasion—conducting official city business inside of his office—he had taken time off from a busy schedule to inspect a suitcase—that contained $20,000 in cold corrupt cash for favors.

As town mayor he had officially solicited and accepted more than $48, 000 in cash, airline tickets, hotel accommodations and other perks.

On one occasion he had confided that he looked good in an orange necktie, but not an orange suit.

Wearing an orange suit, he has been ordered to serve 44 months in the state penitentiary, in the state of West Virginia.

(Interviewer's note: "Uncle Gus" recalled happenings on the old plantation where he was reared. His master was a "king" man, he said, on whose plantation [he lived on] in Richmond, Virginia.)

"In all the years since the war I cannot forget old massa. He was good and kind. He never believed in slavery but his money was tied up in slaves and he didn't want to lose all he had... I know I will see

him in heaven and even though I have to walk ten miles for a bite of bread I can still be happy to think about the good times we had. I am a Confederate veteran but my house burned up wid the medals and I don't get a pension."

—Gus Brown, former slave, WPA interview in the 1930s.

(The interviewer left him sitting with his little pack and a long fork in his hands; and in his eyes, dimmed with age, [was] a far-off look and a tear of longing, for the Old Plantation.)

Yes, and a far-off look and a tear of longing for the old plantation, can be seen in the eyes of most Negro politicians, too!

Negro Politician Jack Johnson...!
Prince George County, Maryland.

The case burst into the spotlight in November when Johnson and his wife, Leslie, 59, now a member of the County Council, were arrested at their brick colonial in Mitchellville. The couple was overheard on an FBI wiretap plotting to hide $79,600 in cash in Leslie Johnson's bra and underwear and flush a $100,000 check from a developer down the toilet as federal agents knocked at the door, court papers say... Both Johnsons were charged with evidence tampering, and Jack Johnson was later indicted on bribery and corruption charges.

—Ruben Castaneda and Miranda S. Spivack, Washington Post.

Daniel Colton, a developer, was a man on a mission: he needed *help*, inside help, on a large-scale project that could be cash in the bank for his business. Fishing the waters of City Hall, he snared the biggest perch in the pool:

Jack Johnson, a country executive, would later stand accused of steering millions of dollars in government funds to his developer friend, and for accepting campaign contributions and mortgage payments in exchange for a bit of… influence peddling.

An investigation by The Washington Post found that Johnson had awarded 51 county contracts totaling more than $3 million to 15 friends and supporters; that in some cases he had gone over the heads of the members of the County Council to place cronies into county jobs; and that he created city jobs and staffed them with friends and fraternity brothers; who had little or no experience in their made-up jobs.

Johnson under the glare of flashing cameras, admitted that he and other public officials had come into cash, airline tickets, and campaign and mortgage payments, in ways that weren't… very ethical.

Prosecutors said the former county executive had steered millions of dollars in government funds to developers in exchange for bribes; that he had used his authority to rig liquor store hours in favor of a store-owner who, behind closed doors, had slipped him some moola for his efforts, that he had aided a corrupt cop and had channeled city business to a certain… developer. He had also been accused of securing jobs for members of his faithful inner circle.

"This was not a single act of bribery," the presiding judge said. "This was not a mistake. This was not a simple wrong turn. [This is something that] puts the country on a path to being a kleptocracy!"

Initially, Johnson had asserted his innocence and had vowed to fight tooth and nail to clear himself, but shortly afterwards, he agreed to a plea deal; in which he pled guilty to extortion, and witness and evidence-tampering.

On December 6, 2011, Johnson's tooth and nail fight ended when he was sent to the Big House. To serve seven years and three months; for crimes against the citizens of Prince George County, Maryland.

After the surrender, some po' white trash tried to make us take some land. They say you is "titled to vote in the elections and to have money same as they, but most of us didn't pay no attention to 'em…

I ain't never associated with no trashy niggers… I am goin' to be a good nigger to the last."

—Matilda Pugh Daniel, former slave, WPA interview in the 1930s.

Negro politician to his Ol Massa: I is goin' to be a good nigger, to de last, Massa.

Negro Politician Kevin White…!

Hillsborough County, Florida

The men first met with Hillsborough County Commissioner Kevin White and his father in January 2010… They had $1,000 in cash and a desire to win a tow-truck permit… White, who was chairman of the agency that regulates wreckers, said their application should "sail through."

What was not known to Kevin White at that moment was that he was dealing with an undercover FBI agent, and that their conversation was being video-taped.

The videotape shows White sitting in the passenger's seat of a car as the driver, an undercover FBI agent sits behind the steering wheel telling White, "I want to take care of you for taking care of me. Now you said you needed ten and I'm going to give you five." White, who appears severely let down, utters, "Oh man," as he stuffs the money into his pocket.

White's father, Gerald, a former politician who served time in prison, appeared to have masterminded the scheme. He had let it be known that tow companies could get favorable treatment if the price was right.

An informer told Gerald in March of 2010 that he would be submitting a permit request to the PTC. He said that he would be using the name, Tri-County Auto Towing, Inc. But the company would be registered in someone else's name. The following month an undercover agent using the name, Darryl was introduced to Gerald's son, Kevin White, and the permit was approved two months later. Kevin had hinted to the undercover agent that he needed $10,000 for his election campaign, and that his application would be "walked through" with no problem.

White, at trial, as he stood before the judge awaiting his decision, had implied that it was his father who had led him down the path to perdition.

He had been born out of wedlock.

And he had never known his father, a politician, with a prison record.

"I always wanted a relationship with my father," he tearfully told the courtroom. "…But I *see* where that's gotten me…"

It got him a prison sentence, 300 hours of community service, and a fine of $7,500.

I knew Jerry Lawson, who was Justice of Peace. He was a nigger, a low-down devil. Man, them niggers done more dirt in this city. The Republicans had this city and state. I knew several of them niggers—Mack Armstrong, he was Justice of Peace. I can't call the rest of them. Nothing but old thieves. If they had been people, they'd been honest. Wouldn't sell their brother. It is bad yet. They still stealin' yet.

—Campbell Armstrong, former slave; interviewed in the 1930s by the WPA.

They were stealing then, and they are really stealing now.

Chapter Nine
Plantation Patrolling Negro Cops

The slaves was glad to be free so they could come and go jus' like white folks, and not have the patroller gittin' them. They was tired of being beat up and if they run away, the Sheriff was after them, and he would beat them

—Henry Lewis McGaffey, former slave, interviewed in the 1930s by the WPA.

No institution on earth outside of slavery has retarded the growth of the Black race more so than the Plantation Patrollers that are also known as the Police.

And reading the words of the old-time slave, Henry Lewis McGaffey, one gets the sneakiest suspicion: that the Black man's very intimate relationship with the Police, is not one of those beautiful once-in-a-lifetime romances that sprung up suddenly overnight, but one that through bad times and worse times has always been there, at the beck and call… of the White Ruling Class.

Slave patrols and Night Watches, which later became modern police departments, were both designed to control the behaviors of minorities… The St. Louis police were founded to protect residents from Native Americans in that frontier city, and many southern police departments began as slave patrols… Slave patrols helped to maintain the economic order and to assist the wealthy landowners

in recovering and punishing slaves who essentially were considered property

> —Victor E. Kappeler, Ph.D., Associate Dean and Foundation Professor, School of Justice Studies; Eastern Kentucky University.

In other words, waving a Negro in front of a sheriff is like waving a sweat-soaked shirt in the face of a salivating, alert-eyed slave-tracking hound; the temptation to attack, interspersed with genes, motive, and opportunity, is just too intense for the sheriff, or the hound, to resist.

This strange fixation on keeping Blacks down and out on the Old Plantation is not endemic to the South alone; for in a large number of Northern cities, where shaking and baking Black suspects who have been stomped and tossed unconscious and un-seat belted into the back of hot police vans, vans that swerve, and weave through traffic at lightning speed, is big sport—more exciting than the Super Bowl—in some quarters—sorta like the old halcyon days when hired plantation patrollers on horseback would lame and hang some poor run-to-ground slave whose only crime was tip-toeing beyond the bounds of the plantation, after curfew.

The literature clearly establishes that a legally sanctioned law enforcement system existed in America long before the Civil War, for the express purpose of controlling the slave population, and protecting the interests of slave owners.

The similarities between the old-time slave patrols, and modern, American policing, are too salient to dismiss or ignore. Hence, the slave patrol should be considered a forerunner of modern American law enforcement

> —Victor E. Kappeler, Ph.D., Associate Dean and Foundation Professor, School of Justice Studies; Eastern Kentucky University.

It could be argued that the first White cop to grace the shores of America was the whip-cracking slave-crippling overseer, and that his legacy lives on (fondly) in the hearts and minds of today's Strong-Arm

Negro Guardian Departments—known in the hood as the never-met-a-Negro-it-didn't-want-to-shoot-on-sight, Police, Department.

"The overseer was death and gall, and that wasn't all. I mean he was pretty mean. He was common white trash... There wasn't any jail... Sometimes they were locked in the gin house of some other farm house."
—Aaron Jones, former slave, interviewed in the 1930s by the WPA.

A system of policing built on tactics developed during slavery, is bound to produce cops who act accordingly, ten times, out of what, ten, perhaps...?

So, when skeptics say that slavery-imitating police brutality reports are overblown—and not nearly as wide spread as bleeding hearts and likeminded crybabies would have us believe, examining this argument inside and out, they would begin to see a disturbing pattern of slave tormenting behavior not only in Southern, or large, over-populated Northern cities, but in towns small and great, all over the entire U. S. map on any wall... in the world.

And that means that the police misconduct on display, today, is nothing new. In cities *throughout* America there are documented cases of law officials beating, planting false evidence, and even murdering, Black folks, almost throughout the entire *history*, of America.

But what is less reported, and less known, is that there are *Negro* cops, who have beaten, planted false evidence, and even murdered... the *Black* folks, that they were *sworn* to protect... And for keeping their brethren in chains on the plantation, an elite group of the Massa's Negro plantation patrollers, indistinguishable from the Massa's *White* plantation patrollers, shall now... be called... by name...

Plantation Negro Cop Len Davis…!

New Orleans, Louisiana

On December 5, 1994, police officer Len Davis was arrested for the murder of Kim Marie Grove (a young mother of three children) in retaliation for a complaint she had filed against the officer with the New Orleans Police Department.

Below is an article written by her daughter that appeared in a September 20, 2020 article in the Louisiana Chapter of the ACLU.

My name is Jasmine Groves and I am the youngest of three children of Kim Marie Groves. A former New Orleans police officer Len Davis put a hit on my mother in retaliation for her witnessing him beat a teenager in our neighborhood and filing a complaint against him. The day my mother reported Officer Davis was the day before my 13th birthday. About 3:30pm, she called the office to file the complaint, and it usually took 24 to 72 hours for an officer to be notified of a complaint against them. Unfortunately, Davis knew within hours of my mother filing the complaint; by the time she made it home that night, the hit to take her life was already set.

Because it was the night before my birthday, my mom was planning my party. My cousin and I were having a sleepover, and we were playing cards. My mom came into the room and started singing "happy birthday to you, happy birthday to you." I smiled the whole time she sang because she always made me feel special. For some crazy reason, it felt like she knew she would not get to wish me a happy birthday the next day. After she walked out of the door, within seconds, the phone rang. I was always the one to run to answer it, but that time I wish I hadn't. As I said hello, all I heard was a woman voice screaming into the phone, "Kim has just been shot and I think she's dead!"

At that moment, my heart stopped, I was stiff. I could not think, I could not talk, I was stuck. I was wishing she'd say "She had it wrong; it was a mistake." I dropped the phone and ran screaming

to my family. As we all ran out of the door, we saw my mother's body lying in the street, lifeless, her eyes still open. She had the biggest hole in her head that you could see straight through it, her brains were on the ground next to her. As people consoled us, my grandfather picked up her brains, brought it to the levee, and placed it into the water. I took that as him setting her free, and accepting that she was not going to make it. As I dialed 911 for help, it took them forever.

This Negroistic tale of murder, drugs, and mayhem was slammed into high-gear when a drug-dealer named Terry Adams told the FBI that he was being extorted for thousands of dollars by Black New Orleans police officers.

The FBI opened a sting operation called Operation Shattered Shield, where undercover agents, paid corrupt police officers to stand guard outside of buildings where cocaine deals were transpiring.

When Davis, one of the crooked cops who were under investigation by the FBI, learned that Groves had lodged an eight-page civil rights complaint against him (that was supposed to remain confidential) he quickly hired a triggerman, a drug dealer named Paul Hardy.

Shortly after Kim Groves had wished her daughter a Happy Birthday, Hardy approached Groves as she stood on a nearby sidewalk, and shot her point-blank in her head, execution style.

Known in the community as "Robocop" due to his large size and his aggressive policing style, Len Davis had a reputation as both a good *and* bad cop. He had been suspended six times and received 20 complaints between 1987 and 1992.

When Davis heard that his accuser had been shot, he jumped up and down in celebration and shouted: "Yeah, yeah, yeah, rock, rock-a-bye!" Later, he would jubilantly tell one of his fellow cops-in-crime, "Signal 30, NAT," police code for "necessary action taken."

But his jubilation was short-lived.

Soon afterwards he was found guilty of depriving Kim Groves of her civil rights, and a judge took the appropriate, necessary action, to sentence a Negro, to death-row.

In 2018, the city of New Orleans settled a lawsuit that granted Groves' three children $1.5 million.

Jasmine Groves, who was 12 years old when her mother was murdered, says she thinks of her mother constantly, and still considers her to be her best friend. And every year as her birthday approaches, she holds a memorial service with family members to help her cope with the loss of a very dear best friend, who, she says, "will never live to see her grandchildren."

Plantation Negro Cop Vancito Gumbs…!

Atlanta, Georgia

On May 16, 2019, Black police officer Vancito Gumbs was sentenced to 15 years in prison, followed by five years of supervised release, on RICO conspiracy charges.

A full-time police officer, and part time hired killer for the Gangster Disciples, Gumbs had caught the attention of his police supervisors when they received a complaint that he was using illegal drugs. When he was questioned, his interrogators were gaped-mouth stunned when he quickly admitted to "killing people, as a hit-man, for the Disciples."

The prosecutors in the case said that Gumbs (whose membership in a gang of thugs that had vowed to run the United States if its government failed) had disgraced this uniform, and had abused his power—as a police officer—for adding a gang that had destroyed, and ended, innocent lives.

Over the course of his trial the jury would hear evidence that gang members had shot a total of 24 people, and that one victim had been left to die in front of a 4-year-old child. And one of the survivors had been shot more than a dozen times.

His defense team had argued that Gumbs was simply an innocent, wanna-be thug, who had had no involvement in the killings, and shootings., but a wire-tap had proved beyond doubt that he *had* been a very active participant, and had given gang-leaders inside information about the types of crimes the police were investigating. He had also sent a text message to the mother of one of his children, blatantly admitting his role as a hit-man, for the Gangster Disciples.

After four years in federal custody, Gumbs, in leg chains, was finally led into the courtroom of US District Judge Thomas W. Thrash Jr., and was sentenced to serve 15 years in a federal prison.

Dekalb County Police Chief James Conroy, at a news conference, said that he was saddened to hear the news that one of his *finest* officers had been involved in such a long list of criminal activities.

"There are bad apples in every organization," he said, and in what has to be one of the greatest understatements of all times. He added: "And *this*... was a *bad* apple."

Plantation Negro Cop Sidney Dorsey...!
DeKalb County, Georgia

As Sidney Dorsey, the Black, former sheriff of DeKalb County, sat in a crowded courtroom on the tenth of July in 2002, charged with the murder of his Black political rival, Derwin Brown, Dorsey's staunch supporters absolutely *refused* to believe that he could be guilty. This they believed was a set-up, orchestrated by Dorsey's political enemies.

Derwin Brown had been a longtime county police officers, and as he had campaigned for Dorsey's job had promised to put an end to the scandals that had plagued the sheriff's department for decades.

Dorsey had become the county's first Black sheriff four years earlier. He had previously been arrested on a manslaughter charge and for domestic abuse but by and large his victory had been hailed in the Black community as a giant step towards justice, and equality, in a racist part of the country were there was little justice, or equality, for Black folks.

When he was sworn in as the county's first Black sheriff, a few eyebrows were raised when reports surfaced that some of the corruption that had plagued the sheriff's department in previous administrations were plaguing the department in Dorsey's administration; but when Derwin Brown was assassinated, shortly before replacing Dorsey, Dorsey's supporters stood firmly behind him refusing to believe that anyone, would be so brazen as to assassinate his rival two days before he was to be sworn in as the new sheriff.

But at his trial, as witnesses took the stand and stated unequivocally that Dorsey had ordered the hit on Derwin Brown, even Dorsey's most rabid supporters began to have serious doubts about his innocence.

Two of those witnesses were former sheriff's deputies David Ramsey and Melvin Walker, who had been given immunity for their testimony. Walker had testified that on the night shortly after Derwin Brown had returned from a party celebrating his graduation from a sheriff's training course, he had stepped from the shadows and pumped 11 rifle bullets into Brown's back after he had exited his car and stepped across his yard towards the front porch of his house.

Under oath, Ramsey and Brown testified that Sidney Dorsey had ordered the hit, with Walker serving as the triggerman after the men had drawn straws.

But the defense countered by placing the blame solely on the two former deputies, arguing that they had been granted immunity for their false testimony.

But as the trial neared its end, even Dorsey's most fervent supporters had to admit that the case against their sheriff seemed… iron-clad. And when Superior Court Judge Cynthia Becker sentenced Dorsey to life on the murder charge, and an additional 23 years on racketeering and a violation of oath of office charge, there were *loud* cheers, but *no* quiet protests—from the other side of the courtroom.

Plantation Negro Cop Robert Faulcon Junior…!

New Orleans, Louisiana

In the early hours of August 29, 2005, a water-logged levee surrounding the city of New Orleans, collapsed, with a loud explosion, and in less than 25 minutes the Gulf of Mexico swept over the breached levee and poured 14 feet of floodwaters into the nearby mostly Black neighborhoods; sending residents fleeing for their lives.

The 911 switchboard was swamped with calls from desperate citizens pleading for help. Television cameras in helicopters captured people stranded on the rooftops of homes, parents sloshing in chest high waters floating babies in plastic buckets, old people in the arms of loved ones searching for higher ground, and abandoned, half-submerged vehicles, with dead, bloated bodies floating among the wreckage.

Hours earlier, city officials had ordered a mass evacuation, and as highways clogged with citizens fleeing the city in droves, it was plainly evident that there were thousands of stranded New Orleans who had been left behind to fend for themselves.

The police officers who had not fled for higher ground were tasked with two missions: To save the residents who had been left behind, and to prevent thieves from looting.

Ronald Madison, a mentally challenged 40-year-old Black man, and his brother, Lance, were crossing the Danziger Bridge to return to a hotel, where they had sought shelter after being flooded out of their home earlier, when an unmarked state police car drove up and screeched to a loud stop.

Reports of gunfire from looters had been reported in the area and the cops were there to investigate.

Suddenly, more gunshots rang out.

But these were not the gunshots of looters, they were the gunshots of the police officers; as they took aim, and opened fire on a crowd of refuges crossing the bridge.

As loud screams and chaos erupted on the bridge, the two Madison brothers fled for cover, but the two cops in state police cars fell in line behind them.

As the white cop in the police car indiscriminately opened fire on the fleeing crowd, the Black officer, Robert Faulcon Jr. carefully raised his shotgun, took careful aim, and blasted Ronald Coleman in his back as he ran away.

With Ronald crying, in pain, he implored his brother to tell his mother that he loved her.

Ronald's brother would later testify in court that one of the officers then rushed up and kicked Ronald and asked a nearby cop if he was one of the shooters.

Adding insult to injury, Lance, the brother, was roughly taken into custody and was falsely charged with eight counts of attempting to kill police officer. And he would be held in custody for three weeks, before finally being released with no charges filed.

In the coming weeks and months, the police would set out to invent witnesses, plant phony evidence, conjure up fictional reports, and create a public relations campaign portraying the officers as heroes. And in a show of brotherly support, police officials would rally around the White cops, involved in the incident, stating that only bullets from the Black cops had hit their targets.

The autopsy report would later reveal that Ronald Madison, a mentally impaired man who had been hesitated to leave the rapidly flooding home of his brother—because of his concern for the safety of his dog—had sustained seven gunshot wounds; five of them in his back.

A federal jury would later find a total of five police officers guilty of killing two civilians, injuring five others, willfully violating their civil rights, and false prosecution. And another cop would be convicted later for helping to cover up the killings.

Faulcon had testified that he had been filled with "indescribable fear" [of the fleeing refugees] at the time of the shooting, but the judge was not moved.

For the crime of being terrified of a fleeing crowd, and back-shooting a mentally impaired Black man, Faulcon was sentenced to serve 65 years with like-minded Negroes…in prison.

Plantation Negro Cops, Evodio Hendrix, Jemell Rayan, Marcus Taylor, Maurice Ward, and Momodu Gando…!

Baltimore, Maryland

Black police officers Evodio Hendrix, Jemel Rayan, Marcus Taylor, Maurice Ward, and Momodu Gando, had come up with a master plan that couldn't fail.

They would engage in home-invasions, then steal drugs from drug dealers, and sell them on the streets.

The narcotics officers had convinced themselves that street-level crime, for criminal, like them, was the surest short-cut (that they could think of) to success, and promotion.

In March of 2017, the five Black Baltimore police officers along with three White police officers were charged with racketeering, robbery, extortion, and overtime fraud, after DEA agents had heard officer Gondo admitting to selling drugs on a taped recording.

Black detective Momodu Gondo eventually admitted to providing protection and information to a heroin dealer, and during the trial admitted that he and another officer had planned a burglary using police tracking devices, to tell them when their victims were not at home. He also admitted that he had stolen 800 grams of heroin, a gun, and expensive jewelry. And he also admitted that he had stolen cash from people's homes and had split the proceeds with fellow officers. And in a brazen act of audacity, he told a fellow officer not to get greedy, because they could commit similar crimes "three times a year."

Black detective Evodio Hendrix admitted to stealing money on traffic stops, and while executing search warrants. He said that he was instructed by White ring-leader Jenkins to carry a BB gun in his squad car in case it was needed to get himself out of a situation like shooting an unarmed suspect.

Black officer Jemell Rayan admitted to being a *thief* before joining the police department, and admitted to stealing $20,000 during a home invasion. He also admitted to stealing drugs and splitting the take with Officer Jenkins, his crime partner.

Black officer Maurice Ward also confessed to swiping money during police stops and while executing search warrants. He also stated that his fellow rogues in blue had stolen over $100,000 from a safe, but the haul was so large that he got scared and tossed the loot into a field behind his house. "It was just too much," he said, "the good outweighed the good…"

Black detective Marcus Taylor was the youngest officer in the gang and testified that their main method of making false arrests was what he called "door pops." Busting in doors as though they were imitating an arrest warrant, and chasing down anyone that ran from the scene.

Taylor was also found guilty in a number of other robberies, including the theft of $100,000 from drug traffickers.

The thugs with dirty police-badges apparently believed that victimizing criminals and stealing their ill-gotten gains was not such a bad thing, who was going to complain, so what the heck. Go for it.

At trial the Judge *went* for it, and sentenced the misguided miscreants to long much-deserved prison terms.

Plantation Negro Cops, Schonton Harris, Kelvin Harris, and James Archibald…!

Miami, Florida

To the people who knew her, Schonton Harris was just your ordinary hard-working cop—who had a special place in her heart for the people she served. She had been trained in a crisis intervention program that dealt with the mentally ill, and had been a member of the prestigious Miami Police Department's Honor Guard.

At the Winn-Dixie supermarket where she worked as a security guard in her spare time, she was well-respected by those she came into contact with, and no one in their wildest dreams would have suspected her of being a rogue cop; who would *kill* for the drug dealers that she had been hired to protect.

What most folks didn't realize, however… was that there was a dark side… to the friendly cop, who was always there; in time of *need*?

On New Year's Day in 2009, according to her personnel file, Harris had approached a man playing fetch with his dog in a park. She asked the man to leash the dog. When the dog approached her and she was told that the dog only wanted to sniff her; she un-holstered her service revolved, took aim, and fired point blank at the dog's head.

But this was one of her… *minor*, offenses. She had also been investigated for use of force, 24 times.

When the FBI got wind of Harris's part time duty— as a full-time partner—with some rather unsavory drug smugglers—they quickly enlisted the help of fellow Miami police officer, Catina Anderson, who agreed to act as a confidential informant and wear a recording device.

Anderson was told to approach Schonton about providing delivery of some drug money belonging to drug dealers. Her cousin, she said, needed protection: he had a large supply of Percocet pills in his car and he needed someone to stand guard as he delivered drug money to a bank.

Schonton accepted the offer.

Schonton was then introduced to an undercover FBI agent who claimed to be a member of an East Coast cocaine trafficking operation. The operation was growing and needed to transport several kilos of cocaine to different locations, and needed "an army of people" for protection.

Schonton recruited another Miami Officer, James Archibald, who told her that he was "all in" on the deal, and the three cops met with the undercover FBI agent to discuss two 20-kilograms cocaine shipments.

The FBI agent paid the cops $2,500 for their help, and arranged for a sting operation in which the officers would pick up a large supply of cocaine at a local boat marina, and transport the dope to two locations in Miami. The three cops were paid $4,000 for their cooperation, and was told to stand by, and that other money-making deals were in the works.

But if the three cops were dreaming of golden deals, what they *got* was silvery handcuffs, and an armed police escort to the local jail.

At trial, Schonton pled guilty to conspiracy to possess with the intent to distribute cocaine, and was sentenced to 15 and a half years behind steely gray bars in prison, while Kelvin Harris and James Archibald were convicted of conspiracy to possess with the intent to distribute cocaine, attempted possession with intent to distribute cocaine and possession of a firearm in furtherance of a drug trafficking crime, and were sentenced to 27 years and 10 years, behind those same steely bars, respectively.

Plantation Negro Cops, Tadarrius Bean, Demetrius Haley, Emmitt Martin III, Desmond Mills Jr. and Justin Smith…!

Memphis, Tennessee

On the night of January 7, 2023, 29-year-old Tyre Nichols, a Fed-X worker and the father of a 3 year old boy, was returning to his home from a nearby park, when he was pulled over by 5 Black police officers for reckless driving. According to the reports submitted to their supervisors, the cops stated that Mister Nichols had been observed driving erratically, became combative when questioned, fled the scene and was apprehended a few blocks away.

Case closed.

But… cameras… on nearby telephone… poles told an entirely different story.

The truth-telling video showed grainy black and white images of Nichols being drugged from his car and slammed to the ground and pummeled for no apparent reason.

When the 5 officers were quickly arrested and charged with murder the community was outraged.

An NBC TV reporter asked a local resident what flashed to his mind, when he saw TV images of five Black cops beating the life out of a fellow Black citizen, and he had this to say:

"Some of these officers get behind their badges and forget where they came from. Some came from rough neighborhoods, too. But some of them take that power, and misuse it. They didn't come to my neighborhood and pull no cats out of trees. They came over when we were little boys, 13, 14 years old, and roughed us up. And for no reason."

And there were others in the community who expressed similar sentiments.

"A lot of times," another frustrated neighbor said, "it's the Black officers who beat us worse than the white officers."

A study conducted by Michigan State University, and the University of Maryland, found that Black police officers were more likely to kill Black civilians than White civilians. The study also found that the Hispanic and other minority police officers were more inclined to shoot member of their own race than members of other races.

But was it simply peer pressure that had driven those Black cops to commit murder, and photograph their victim as he lay dying on a dark lonely street in the hood?

Were those 5 officers so anxious to prove themselves worthy of their fellow White officers' occasional pat on their heads that even their victim's cries for his mother's help, were ignored?

Some critics of law enforcement, believe that peer-pressure, the overwhelming desire to bond with their fellow White officers, is the driving factor behind these black cop/black shooting victim cases.

But the mother of Tyre Nichols has precious little time to figure out the whys and the wherefore. She simply has this to say to the men who shot her boy: "People don't know what those five police officers did to our family. They have brought shame to their own families. They have brought shame to the Black community. I just feel sorry for them. I really do. Because they didn't have to do this."

Negro police officers Tadarrius Bean, Demetrius Haley, Emmitt Martin III, Desmond Mills Jr. and Justin Smith, didn't have to *do* what they did.

But their Plantation Negro DNA, *made* them… *do* it.

Chapter Ten
Plantation Negro Entertainers

The following is a radio interview with Bill Perry, a former FBI informant.

Interviewer: You were active in the infiltration of a number of social groups. How much research and study, did the FBI engage in, of Black culture in the late sixties?

Bill Perry: A great amount.

Interviewer: Give me an idea.

Bill Perry: They have a file on every type of magazine that Blacks read; they have a file on the music. Dance. Theatre; actors; comedians, you name it.

Interviewer: And they would actively study these…?

Bill Perry: Oh yes. Oh yes, definitely… They make in-depth analysis of the people they're dealing with, culturally. You can take the culture, and use it against them…

Interviewer: Tell me about some of the various cultural organizations that you infiltrated, what you did?

Bill Perry: … Watts Writer's workshop… which was one of the oldest established Black Writer's Workshops.

Interviewer: But that place burned down.

Bill Perry: Yeah. The Bureau had it burned down. I know because I participated. I did the arson. But I don't want to talk about this Cointel. I want to talk about the Black Desk. The Black Desk was set up to infiltrate Black organizations, and Black groups.

To monitor social activities, social unrest, cultural groups and such, in the Black community.

Interviewer: And it still exists [the Black Desk]…?

Bill Perry: As far as I know, yes…

"You can take the culture, and use it against them… You can take the culture, and use it against them… You can take the culture, and use it against them…"

Taking the Black man's culture, and using it against him, is one of the cleverest, most successful schemes ever devised by man to be used against man: a time-tested, very cunning strategy, that was just as effective *during* slavery as it is today.

Ol Massa's first attempt at using the Black man's culture against himself was the creation of a cartoon character called Sambo. Sambo was the plutocratic slave-owner's idea of the perfect slave. Childish, first and foremost, but he was also plumb tickled to be the footstool of his masters; he was docile, and so lazy that if not for the kindness of his betters who had to hand feed him, he would've starved for lack of ambition; oh, and yes, he was loyal. And devoted. And would die to remain enslaved.

A foot-shuffling watermelon-eating fool, Sambo was the personification of the perfect Black male. And all during slavery he was pictured in white children's storybooks and on their lunch boxes and in their schoolbooks so that a whole generation of future masters and mistresses would come to see the Negro as their inferior, and as a poor, wretched, only half civilized ape-like creature, that would henceforth, and forever be in need of the white man's protection.

Ol Massa's second attempt at creating the perfect Black male was the creation of the Jim Crow character.

Jim, the ideal Negro for the turbulent Order rearranging years of Reconstruction, was the soothing anecdote for a nation wondering what to do with so many freed Negroes on its hands. Jim like his cousin Sam was childish, first and foremost, but he was also plumb tickled to be the poster child of the KKK; he was docile, and so lazy that if not for the kindness of his former masters, who had to assist him in stealing watermelon, he would have starved for lack of ambition; oh, and yes, he was loyal, to his pursuers, and devoted to his torturers, and would die to hang on a tree.

In 1828, a white struggling actor named Thomas Dartmouth Rice witnessed a Black man dancing in the streets, but the thing that really caught his attention was the song he was singing.

"Come listen all you galls and boys.

I'm going to sing a little song,

My name is Jim Crow;

Weel about and turn about and do jis so,

Eb'ry time I weel about I jump Jim Crow."

Rice blackened his face with burnt cork, appeared on stage, and became an overnight success.

He took his minstrel show on the road all across America and Europe. His Jim Crow character was so popular that in time it not only became the embodiment of the Black male, but the face of the separate-but-equal laws enacted in the 1890s.

Rice had watered a seed that had been implanted into the subconsciousness of America since Colonial times: that the Black race was a lazy, sub-human race, and was totally underserving of the rights and dignity accorded the white man: And this old image, this old seed that will never die, is—and will always be—as American, as apple pie.

"Sometimes I thinks I sleeps too much muhself. I ain't go open thet do', so lazy-like I can't git all my sleep. I rest all night, 'n sleep in the daytime. But in the afternoon, when I really needs to relax, I jest seem ta toss 'n turn."

—Steppin' Fetchit, from the movie, *Lazy Richard.*

Lincoln Andrew Perry was born in 1902 and became the first Negro actor to become a millionaire catering to the bigotry of white people. Perry, who was born to West Indian parents and was rumored to have a negative opinion about American Blacks seemed to take keen delight in portraying the servile, foot-shuffling, Jim Crow character, called Steppin' Fetchit.

In the 1930s and '40s, as Black Americans were being lynched and totally excluded from the broader society, Steppin' Fetchit was the go-to Negro that white Hollywood producers turned to when scripts landed on their desks calling for an actor who spoke the language of the average Black man on the street. When Hollywood big-shots needed a Negro, who embodied the heart and soul of the average Black man, Steppin' Fetchit answered the call.

"Feet don't fail me now," became the words any self-respecting Black man would utter when confronted with ghosts, and "I rest all night 'n sleep in the daytime, became his trifling do-nothing lament when someone knocked on his door with a job-offer. And white America lapped him up like kids licking candy."

In the late 1940s Steppin' Fetchit's star was fading. The subservient toe-twinkling Jim Crow character in the movies had not completely disappeared from the silver screen, but more intelligent, sophisticated Black performers were making themselves known: and actors like Ethel Waters and Eunice Wilson and Paul Robeson were beginning to appear in a variety of roles normally associated with white performers. Although they often performed in scenes with cotton patches and watermelons as backdrops, their dignity and grace transcended the demeaning context in which they appeared and in time the door they opened swung wide enough for actors like James Edwards, Sidney Poitier and Harry Belafonte (Black men who refused to surrender their manhood) to make their debut.

But Hollywood in the 1970s woke up to a *whole* new world. It was the age of Black Power; and Vietnam, and the hippie anti-Establishment movement. Shock-waves had swept through the spines of the nation's power-brokers and at their wits end trying to contain what could become a mass nasty uprising, spoon-fed the American psyche with movies that glorified drugs, with thuggish bad-acting Blacks in the starring roles.

Hollywood slapped in the face with reality had realized that the changing times called for a major change in their aging, champion watermelon eating white-butt-licking stooge. Yes it was sad but true: Old Jim was in desperate need of a major, *major*, overhaul, the boy needed a massive face-lift that couldn't wait. One that was not only appropriate, for the *times,* but one that *reflected,* the times?

And drug dealers who beat The Man at his own game, suddenly made a spectacular appearance on the silvery screen, and the flashy, fur-coat wearing Black drug-pusher was now the personification of the average, hard-working, Black man.

In the 1990s, the Black Drug Negro with minor adjustments was very easily transformed into the… Black Thug, Negro.

And: "Shot my momma! Shot my daddy! Shot my old aunt Hattie!" became his signature, calling card.

The perfect embodiment of the '90s New Plantation Negro, Thug Negro, was Ol Massa's crowning achievement.

He had created a Negro that put all the other Negroes he had created to shame. His Thug Negro, his kill-crazy self-cannibalizing Negro, was joy to his eyes, and money in his bank—when government-sanctioned private prisons, became the hot new *stock*—for the astute investor?

A multi-faceted Negro Thug Negro embodied all of the attributes of his predecessor the Drug Negro: prone to violence, he was still as dumb as a brick, but he was now a whirling twirling Uzi-toting Tasmanian devil.

But as out of style as he had become, Hollywood wasn't about to give up on a good thing, like Jim. The Jim Crow Negro character had lowly but sho'ly shown white audiences world-wide the true nature of the Black man, and white producers, were not about to give up on a *sure* thing; like Jim.

During the 1980s and on into the nineties, with Jim in mind, Ol Massa gave us the Jim Crow big mouthed Sambo-like character, J. J., on Good Times: and America went nuts when he rolled his wild white eyes and shook his kinky head and screamed, Dy-no-mite!

The Negro judge on the TV show, Laugh-In gave the nation one belly contorted chuckle after the other with his, "Here comes de Judge, here comes de Judge, routine (and the show's recurring phrase, sock it to me, sock it to me, was coined by Steppin' Fetchit, in the 1945 musical Big Timers)."

Starsky and Hutch gave us a Negro pimp that looked like a flashing jive-walking neon-lighted escapee from a lunatic asylum.

And who can forget lovable little Arnold on Different Strokes: "Whatchu talkin' 'bout, Willis?"

In the Nineties Ol Massa gave us Homeboys from Outer Space, a parody of Star Trek. The opening shot shows two young homies whirling through outer space on a cartoonish space-craft, as the announcer, solemnly intones: "Space. What a *cool* place. These are the voyages of Morris Clay and Tiberius Walker. Their ongoing mission? To seek out new life-forms. And sleep with them."

As the twenty-first century made its debut, ABC Television debuted, Blackish. The show opens with a scene showing a highly successful Negro giving us a tour of his lovely Negro home. In his Negro closet we see 50 pairs of Air Jordan's and a wide array of garish looking baseball caps, the fruit, and symbols of his Negro success. He wants his family to be Black, not Blackish, and apparently the only way he can make his family Black, is to transform them into Negroes, with all the stereotypical trappings of the Negro lifestyle.

And right-thinking Blacks who were rightly Black were rightly outraged:

ABC Television executives were delivered the following petition, a petition that had been signed by over one million concerned parents and ordinary Americans:

"We are signing this petition in hopes that ABC will reconsider airing its new sitcom 'Black-ish' this fall. We find it racist, socially damaging and offensive based on its concept that stereotypical black people are less {human] than others, that hip hop culture is all blacks are supposed to embrace, and that culture and race are one and the same.

This series is damaging and offensive for the following reasons:

1. It perpetuates the stereotype that culture is solely derived from your ethnicity and not your personal experience. Giving the impression that race is a natural indicator of behavior and continuing the outdated beliefs of racial divisions.

2. Its ridiculous title gives the impression that unless you're a racial stereotype, you're someone less than your race.

3. It gives the impression that black people are only "black" if they embrace the negative stereotypes of hip hop culture.

4. It gives the impression that non stereotypical behavior is an attempt to be another race, and discourages minorities from rising above negative/stereotypical expectations.

5. It continues the damaging tradition of minorities only being on TV is they're talking about being minorities. In 2014 we should be beyond color on TV. Do shows with white leads base their stories around being white?

6. It perpetuates the damaging "one drop" rule, that if someone is of biracial heritage, they must only adhere to the stereotypical behavior of the minority side of their background, rather than not basing their behavior on their race at all.

7. It will inevitably lead to minority children who don't live in or come from stereotypical backgrounds, to be ridiculed and made fun for not adhering to stereotypical behavior.

In 2015, the reality-based show, All My Babies Mamas, highlighting the Negro lifestyle of rapper Shawty Lo and the mamas of his ten babies was Ol Massa's way of showing the world the true Black family; but unexpectedly, was cancelled, due to a mass outpouring of public scorn.

A petition by Color of Change accused the show's producers of exploiting inaccurate, dehumanizing, and harmful perceptions of Black families. The petition went on to state that: Research shows that inflammatory images like these can result in real world consequences for our families, including harsher sentencing by judges, lower likelihood of being hired or admitted to schools, lower odds of getting loans, and a higher likelihood of getting shot by police.

Empire, starring Terrence Howard, debuted in 2015, on Fox TV, detailing the travails of a hip-hop music mogul. The lead character of course is a former Drug Thug whose life is on the rocks as he attempts to cope with a Negro wife, who, surprise, surprise, is an ex-convict, a son who, surprise, surprise, is a rising hip hop star, and another son who, surprise, surprise, is gay and totally emasculated. Just like the average Black family.

Fox TV, the offshoot of twentieth century Movies, coincidentally, is the same outfit that gave us another fine example of Black manhood: are you ready for this? Steppin' Fetchit.

"The practice of racial stereotyping through the use of media has been used throughout contemporary history by various factions in American society to attain various goals," says Steven Gray, Recognizing Stereotypical Images of African Americans in Television and Movies.

He goes on to say that:

"The practice is used most by the dominant culture in this society as a way of suppressing its minority population. The Republican Parties' use of the Willie Horton image in the 1988 Presidential campaign is a small example of how majority groups have used racial stereotyping in the media as a justifiable means to an end. The book Unthinking Eurocentrism by Stam and Shohat supports this notion when they write the functionality of stereotyping used in film demonstrates that they (stereotypes) are not an error in perception but rather a form of social control intended as Alice Walker calls prisons of image... The use of racial stereotyping is destructive to American society on two fronts. First it connotes to the majority population of America that the negative actions of a few minorities sum up the collective values of the whole community... The second effect of stereotyping is that the group being stereotyped begins to internalize the negative images and actually mimic some of the behavior and attitudes portrayed in the negative imagery... One of the most famous examples of internalization of stereotypes is the experiment first used in the case of Brown vs. Brown of Education. In this experiment black children were shown almost identical dolls, the only difference being skin color (one black, one white). When the children were asked which dolls were pretty, nice, smart, clean, etc. child after child pointed to the white doll. However, when asked which doll was ugly, dumb, dirty or evil the black doll was almost always selected."

This is called, brainwashing.

"The pictures that are continuously played before the eyes will eventually permeate the unconscious and begin to direct behavior."
—Dr. Umar Johnson, School Psychologist.

Controlling an individual to the point where he or she will do the bidding of their controllers, against his or her will, is a brainwasher's dream. Brainwashers know that if they can manipulate certain emotional areas of a person's mind they can dictate not only that person's behavior, but his reality.

Black children in today's world are bombarded with violent, and unbelievably negative images—on television and in the movie—that depict Black mothers as welfare queens and Black fathers as missing in action, or proudly unemployed.

Malcolm X speaking from the grave has this to say to those who desire to listen:

"The controlled press... the white press... inflames the white public against Negroes... Once the white public are convinced that most of the Negro community are a criminal element, then this automatically paves the way for the police to move into the Negro community exercising Gestapo tactics; stopping any Black man on the sidewalk, whether he is guilty or whether he is innocent, whether he is well dressed or poorly dressed, whether he is educated or whether he is dumb, whether he is Christian or whether he is Muslim, as long as he is Black, and a member of the Negro community, the white public thinks that the policeman is justified in going in there and trampling on that man's Civil Rights and on that man's human rights. Once the police have convinced the white public that the Negro community is a criminal element, they can go in and question, brutalize, and murder unarmed Negroes, and the white public is gullible enough to back them up. This makes the Negro community a police state. This makes the Negro neighborhood a police state."

Pearls of Wisdom. From the mouth of a man, man enough to be his *own*... man.

"Because you can take the culture, and use it against them…"

Bill Perry, the former FBI informer, had gone on to say that the Bureau was *quite* interested in so called Black radicals, but was *very* interested in the NAACP Image Awards.

The NAACP *Image* Award, did he say? But why would the FBI with its big round eye in the sky be so focused in on such an image-*less*, *innocuous*, event, as the highly ignored Black Image Award.?

"Because you can take the culture, and use it against them…"

In the end, when all has been said and all has been done, the one thing that stands out–like black fly, in a white master's glass of buttermilk–is one irrevocable, indisputable reality:

Ol Massa, the inventor of Sambo and Jim Crow and Drug Negro and Thug Negro, appears to not only have *mastered* the Race Card, upon further examination, he appears to have *invented* the Race Card—long before the Card was known, by name.

"History is a set of lies agreed upon."

—Napoleon Bonaparte.

Chapter Eleven
The Elite Plantation House Negroes

"Back during slavery. There were two kinds of slaves. There was the house Negro and the field Negro.

The house Negroes, they lived in the house with master, they dressed pretty good, they ate good because they ate his food—what he left. They lived in the attic or the basement, but still they lived near the master; and they loved their master more than the master loved himself.

They would give their life to save the master's house quicker than the master would. If the master's house caught on fire, the house Negro would fight harder to put the blaze out than the master would.

If the master got sick, the house Negro would say, 'What's the matter, boss, we sick?' He identified himself with his master more than his master identified with himself. And if you came to the house Negro and said, 'Let's run away, let's escape, let's separate,' the house Negro would look at you and say, 'Man, you crazy. What you mean, separate? Where is there a better house than this? Where can I wear better clothes than this? Where can I eat better food than this?' That was that house Negro. In those days he was called a 'house nigger'. And that's what we call him today, because we've still got some house niggers running around here.

On that same plantation, there was the field, Negro. The Negro in the field caught hell. He ate leftovers. In the house they ate high up on the hog. The Negro in the field didn't get nothing but what

was left of the insides of the hog. They call 'em 'chitt'lin'' nowadays. In those days they called them what they were: guts. That's what you were—a gut-eater. And some of you are still gut-eaters.

The field Negro was beaten from morning to night. He lived in a shack, in a hut; He wore old, castoff clothes. He hated his master.

When the house caught on fire, he didn't try and put it out; that field Negro prayed for a wind, for a breeze. When the master got sick, the field Negro prayed that he'd die.

Just as the slave master of that day used Tom, the house Negro, to keep the field Negroes in check, the same old slave master today has Negroes who are nothing but modern Uncle Toms."

—Malcomb X.

The words above spoken by Malcomb X were written decades ago. But they are even more relevant today than they were then.

In a time when nearly all of the gains that were made by Black folks during the sixties and seventies are under attack by right-wing extremists, we see a wide array of elitist modern-day House Negroes, who are just as devoted to their white benefactors, as their ancestors, and role-models were, in the days of slavery.

In this chapter, we will roll out an X-Ray machine, and delve into the minds of the slinking, light-shunning, knee-shaking, modern-day House Negroes, and try to discern, if it is love of money, or love of power, or if it is simply for the love of their white masters that they stay awake, long into the night, conjuring up plot, after plot, after *plot*, to hold back the advancement of their down-and-out—and fiercely *hated*—fellow sufferers.

And now, to honor those who have chosen to *dishonor* themselves, to salute *their* heroic, boot-licking efforts, to be the *best* House Negroes that money or fame can buy, they shall now be *called...* by name...

House Negro Clarence Thomas...!

Step up to the whipping-post. And take your forty lashes, like a *man*.

In 1991 when Clarence Thomas (a Black man?) was nominated to the Supreme Court to occupy the vacated seat of Thurgood Marshall (a *Black, man*), everything was coming up roses, everything was going swimmingly, going according to plans: Although Thomas had left a slim undetectable snail-like trail as a sitting judge—with only two years of on-the-job training—his ultra-conservative supporters were elated: their man—their *boy*—was a shoo-in: A wealth-enhancing welfare hating Negro loathing Negro that couldn't lose.

But as champagne bottles began popping in offices up and down Wall Street, and as little old ladies began to hold onto their pennies, tightly, on Main Street, Wall Street, *and* Main Street, collectively, were dumbstruck, suddenly: Clarence Thomas, it had been revealed in the newspapers, had made... untoward... advances, toward a certain co-worker, named Anita Hill.

Our boy Clarence Thomas was born in Pin Point, Georgia, on June 23, 1948.

His grandfather had dis-enrolled him from the all-black religious high school he was attending sending him to an all-white Catholic boarding school located in the gentle, genteel aristocracy of Savannah, Georgia.

His classmates, young Sons of the Confederacy, to their credit, did not welcome him with bayoneted rifles, but flowers and bands parading past cheering alumni were also in short supply.

His presence, at the very *white* school, to be blunt, was ridiculed; and somewhat severely at that; in fact, it was one of his class-mate's racist remarks that he overheard about the assassination of Martin Luther King Jr. that had made him change his mind about becoming a priest.

When Thomas attended a conference of Black conservatives in 1980, a columnist for the Washington Post wrote an article about his speech that attracted the attention of the Reagan administration. President Ronald Reagan, who knew a Negro when he saw a Negro, quickly offered Thomas a job as the assistant secretary for civil rights in the Department of Education. Thomas accepted the job and Reagan soon promoted him to head the Equal Employment Opportunity Commission (EEOC)… There, Thomas very quickly changed some very important practices of the EEOC. Under his leadership the agency abandoned the use of timetables and numeric goals, allowing companies more flexibility in their hiring of minorities. Thomas also ended the use of class action suits that relied on statistical evidence of discriminatory effects.

These changes in EEOC practice angered and alarmed many civil rights groups. And made them question, how Thomas, a Black man, could without conscious or any sense of connectedness to his own race align himself with an administration that was as anti-Black as the Reagan administration.

Little did they know that the *words* that had raised the eyebrows of the Washington Post columnist who had written the story that had raised the eyebrows President Reagan, were his attacks on the Evil Welfare State.

In an often-quoted speech that he delivered to that conference of Black conservatives in 1980, Thomas said of his sister, who was then on welfare: She gets mad when the mailman is late with her welfare check. That's how dependent she is. What's worse is that now her kids feel entitled to the check too. They have no motivation for doing better or getting out of that situation.

It was a stunning story.

To hear Thomas tell it, his sister sounded like a classic "welfare queen" of the sort presidential candidate Ronald Reagan had singled out that same year, a painful example of how a well-intended government handout can tie families to a cycle of poverty and dependency.

Unfortunately, Thomas' stunning story… wasn't true.

It turns out that Thomas's sister, the welfare queen, had been deserted by her husband in 1977, and had worked two minimum-wage jobs to support her family. But then she had been forced to stop working to take care of an elderly aunt who had suffered a stroke. And she had had no choice but to go on welfare, for five years, receiving a mere stipend of only $169.00 per month.

But at the time when she was interviews by reporters, she was working as a cook at a hospital where her mother worked as a nurse's assistant.

Her children who had been vilified by Thomas as having been indoctrinated into a cycle of welfare dependency, turned out to be an out and out lie. Her son Mark worked as a carpenter. Her oldest son, Clarence, had enlisted in the Navy and had served aboard the Wisconsin during Operation Desert Storm.

When Anita Hill went to work for the feisty EEOC chairman as his newly appointed assistant it would be safe to assume that she had taken the job thinking that it would be a great boost to her career; but when her boss' behavior took a sudden radical turn toward the wild side, she might have had second thoughts.

Suddenly [according to her Senate Hearings testimony] Thomas began to ask Hill out on dates. He began to whisper about things in graphic details that one does not graphically whisper about in mixed company. And he seemed to have a somewhat... *unusual* fascination... with Coke cans?

When the scandal hit the fan, Republicans were mortified! Their man boy nominee to the Supreme Court, surrounded by natives with pitchforks, could lose his unbiased freedom spreading seat on the Court. Panicking, like cats in a roomful of motorized rocking chairs, his allies launched a ferocious counter attack:

And like a great round eyeball peering through a worldwide magnifying glass Hill's personal life was painstakingly examined, bit, by painstakingly bit, her friends, her lifestyle, her history from the time of her conception was raked through hot coals with a fine-tooth comb.

Her enraged critics painting a picture of her as a nut railed incessantly about her lack of character, about her history as a lover of wild shenanigans, about her hellish determination to bring low a good, and honorable, public servant. Under the glare of flashing cameras, the nation gawking like spectators at a dog-fight the attacks on Hill's character seemed so ferocious at times, that there didn't appear to be one Republican senator, who, for a plug of Southern tobacco, wouldn't have dragged her through the mud, in chains, to the nearest auction block— if the entire proceedings had not be televised.

Senator Orrin Hatch pompously insinuating that she might be working with slick lawyers to derail Thomas' chances of sitting on the High Court was outraged. Simply outraged!

A scourge in the form of a Black Woman was clearly afoot; and in the minds of Thomas's fiercest most loyal supporters something earthshaking had to be done and done as truthfully as ethics permits. If their boy was to survive the stormy onslaught from his deluded critics, he would have to tell *his* side of the story (as truthfully as ethics permitted) and tell it convincingly!

As Thomas commandeered the microphone to defend his honor, the hearings that had captivated the nation were quickly silenced.

"It is a high-tech lynching! For uppity Blacks who think for themselves! And it is a message that unless you kowtow to an old order, this is what will happen to you! If someone wanted to block me because they don't like the composition of the court, that's fine. But to destroy me, senator, I would have preferred an assassin's bullet!"

Ducking and scooting under the table between the legs of his squirming lawyers, he told the committee that Hill's entire testimony was the imaginings of an emotionally disturbed employee, with a very noticeable persecution complex.

He produced imaginary witnesses of his own, silent, invisible witnesses, who under oath swore that they had never stood by and *openly* watched him exhibiting lewd or lascivious conduct towards members of the opposite sex; no; they had watched his lewd lascivious conduct from the windows of their nearby offices; where no one could *see* them.

But as two of Hill's co-workers, fleshly, touchable co-workers, stood behind the curtains waiting to testify that Thomas had crossed the bounds of good taste in their presence as well, a poll taken by CBS found that 58 percent of the respondents believed Thomas; and that only 24 percent believed Professor Hill.

The party was over.

And when the lights above the Senate floor faded to black, Clarence Thomas, a judge whose politics were far, far to the right of the judge he had replaced, became only the second Black man in history to ascend to Supreme Court of the United States of America.

Black America had sympathized with Thomas' high-tech lynching analogy. But if Black America whose empathy Thomas had shamelessly solicited during the hearings expected payment for their loyalty, then Black America was in for a rude punch to the gut: Black America, if it could have peered into the future, would have fastened its seat belts: Its sympathy for a fellow sufferer, was about to be rewarded with a knife in the back and an invite to the doorsteps a sprawling magnolia-scented mansion, near a cotton field. If Thomas's seat on the Supreme Court was anything for the Black race to hoot about the *hooting* was quickly brought to a crashing halt; and Black America was forced to watch in horror as their man on the bench quickly shed his moderate, middle of the road façade, and transformed himself into the very thing that he had been all along—a bobble-eyed far-right extremist. The long contentious Senate Hearings were over, and Clarence Thomas was now the Clarence Thomas that his rich *white* puppet-masters had envisioned, when he spoke passionately all those years ago about his *loving* sisters' crack-like addiction to self-defeating, unnecessary, government handouts.

And America, Black, and white, was now on notice:

A justice whose right-leaning ideology was as pure but not as sane as Justice Anthony Scalia's, ideology, was in the house.

Thomas is not just a member of the conservative block of Supreme Court justices. He is, without doubt, the most conservative justice, willing to regularly strike down long-accepted case law that has been in place for decades, in some cases for as much as a century.

He is the only justice willing to allow states to establish an official religion; the only justice who believes teenagers have no free speech rights at all; the only justice who believes that it is unconstitutional to require campaign funders to disclose their identity; the only justice who believes that truthful tobacco advertising and other commercial speech may not be regulated, even when it is aimed at minors; the only justice who voted to strike down a key provision of the Voting Rights Act; the only justice to say that the court should invalidate a wide range of laws regulating business; and he is the only justice who voted to allow the president to hold American citizens in prison indefinitely without charge and without review by the courts.

Thomas is not a traditional conservative, not the kind of justice who believes that law should be built up incrementally over time and that adhering to workable precedent means the law is predictable and can be relied on. Instead, he, more than any other justice, believes that the court over the past century has gotten large swaths of the law wrong, and that those rulings should be reversed.

—NPR, Nina Totenberg.

Should prisoners be beaten and denied essential medical care?

"I say to myself every day," Thomas had soulfully confessed in his confirmation hearings, "but for the grace of God, there go I. So I can walk in their shoes and I can bring something different to the court."

Two months later, Thomas, now a Supreme Court justice, dissented from a decision upholding an $800 damage award to a prisoner who was beaten so severely by prison guards that his teeth and dental plate were broken. Thomas, joined only by Scalia, said "use of force which causes only insignificant harm to a prisoner… is not cruel and unusual punishment."

Should the voting rights of Blacks be protected?

No, because he believes that laws based on the proportional allocation of political powers according to race should not be tampered with.

Should Affirmative Action, a government hand-out that he accepted, to his everlasting regret, be upheld?

No, because although it is cloaked in good intentions, this form of racial tinkering harms the very people it claims to be helping.

Integration?

In June of 2007 providing the pivotal vote that struck down school integration in Louisville, Kentucky, he sided with the conservative majority: the school had violated the Constitution's guarantee of equal protection.

And in 2021 when Donald Trump asked the Supreme Court to block the turnover of documents to the January 6 House Select Committee, the only justice who sided with Donald Trump, was *slinking*, light-shunning, knee-shaking, good old Uncle Clarence.

And what does he think of Obama being the first Black president of the United States of America?

"The thing that I always knew is that it would have to be a black president who was approved by the elites and the media, because anybody they didn't agree with, they would take apart," he said in a CNN interview.

He went on to say that they had shaken hands at the inauguration, to be polite, but that he had had no in-depth conversation with the President (At Obama's inauguration he had sat with the other justices of the court grinding his jaws and poking out lips and looking as if it was the saddest day of his life).

"It pains me deeply—more deeply than any of you can imagine—to be perceived by so many members of my race as doing them harm," he told a group of lawyers hosted by the National Bar Association. "All the sacrifice, all the long hours of preparation were to help, not to hurt… I have come here today not in anger or to anger."

The room was not impressed. Scattered boos and a few polite hand-claps and he was out of there: lickety-split.

But by all accounts, Thomas believes that history will hail him as a great "prophetic leader of Civil Rights," for fighting a lonely, ostracized, and sometimes fruitless battle: for a truly colorblind America.

If language betrays the mind of the speaker, Thomas' constant lament that he would be taken much more seriously if only he had not benefited from Affirmative Action programs, seems to point to a mind that views itself as a misunderstood victim that has been beaten ragged by a world that does not fully understand him, or the quality, and depth, of his intellect.

But he says he holds no grudges against his critics.

"As a child in the Deep South, I'd grown up fearing the lynch mobs of the Ku Klux Klan; as an adult, I was starting to wonder if I'd been afraid of the wrong white people all along. My worst fears had come to pass not in Georgia but in Washington, D.C., where I was being pursued not by bigots in white robes but by left-wing zealots draped in flowing sanctimony."

After the surrender, some po' white trash tried to make us take some land. They say you is "titled to vote in the elections and to have money same as they, but most of us didn't pay no attention to 'em… I ain't never associated with no trashy niggers… I am goin' to be a good nigger to the last."
—Matilda Pugh Daniel, former slave, WPA interview in the 1930s.

Clarence Thomas, to his rich, white, right-wing handlers: "I's is goin' to be a *good* nigger to the *last*, Massa."

House Negro Dr. Ben Carson...!

Take out your scalpel, and perform a lobotomy on yourself.

Carson was born in Detroit, Michigan, on September 18, 1951.

In his book *Gifted Hands*, he writes: "As a teenager, I would go after people with rocks, and bricks, and baseball bats, and hammers." And in an interview with *Meet the Press* in October 2015, he said he once tried to hit his mother on the head with a hammer, over a clothing dispute.

In the ninth grade, he famously claimed that he tried to stab a friend who had changed the radio station, but the blade broke in his friend's belt buckle. He said the intended victim, whose identity he refused to disclose, was a classmate, but friends, classmates, and neighbors who grew up with him told CNN in 2015 that searching their minds they could not truthfully say that they had witnessed, or had ever heard about the incident.

Carson was later accepted by the Johns Hopkins University School of Medicine neurosurgery program, where he served as a surgical intern; and five years later as a neurosurgery resident.

In February of 2013, he was the keynote speaker at the National Prayer Breakfast, and was an instant hit with the same right-wing conservatives who had welcomed the almost unknown Clarence Thomas into their odious arms, when Thomas had publicly referred to a beloved relative, as a Welfare cheat. In his speech, Carter, taking his cue from the fame and notoriety that Clarence Thomas had achieved condemned President Obama, who was seated less than ten feet away, for his misguided political policies.

After a brief unsuccessful run for president in the 2016 election he joined Trump's transition team as Vice Chairman, and was eventually offered the position of Secretary of Housing and Urban Development, which he eagerly accepted.

The son of a single mother who worked three jobs to support her two children, Carson and his family had relied on housing and food assistance programs to make ends meet. But as Secretary of Housing and Urban Development, he experienced a sudden severe case of amnesia, and set out to curtail the same benefits that he and his family had gladly accepted.

Under the directions of President Trump, one of his first acts in office was to eliminate or attempt to eliminate the Fair Housing regulations that had been designed by the Obama Administration to combat discrimination against Black Americans and other minorities. He would go on to remove protections for transgender people and minorities who live in public housing. And in Trump's four year budget request to Congress he attempted to destroy Community Block Grants for Public Housing, Home Grants, housing vouchers for veterans, the Public Housing Capital Fund, housing grants for Native Americans, and a number of other programs that were designed to revitalize affordable housing for low-income families. And he gladly took part in Trump's effort to eliminate the "disparate impact rule," which states that a person or entity can still be guilty of discrimination even if they're not guilty intentionally, a rule that would make such discrimination lawsuits virtually impossible.

Carson also attempted to delay Obama's Small Area Fair Market Rent (SAFMR) rule, which had been designed to give voucher-holders more options for housing; but the attempt was defeated in court, and the rule remains in place.

And as if all of his groveling attempts to roll back the clock on Civil Rights was not enough, he also proposed rolling back Obama's Equal Access Rule that protects LGBQ and transgender people from being denied access to homeless shelters.

While decimating programs that had been designed to help the poor; Carson, lavishly, spent $31,000 for a dining-room set, for his office, in 2017. *Outraged* and offended that anyone could question his *sterling reputation,* his *devotion* to his people, he quickly outed his wife as the unsavory culprit. But emails revealed that he, *and* his wife, had held hands and willingly assisted in the sleazy affair.

Speaking glowingly of Donald Trump, he said in a Rolling Stone article, that his Ol' Massa was not racist; because people who wash dishes at his gold resort, Mar-a-Lago, *love* him. *Dearly*.

"He's a man who is deeply driven by a sense of kindness and compassion," Carson said with a straight face. "You know, talking to the people who drive the cars and park the cars at Mar-a-Lago, they *love* him—the people who wash the dishes—because Ol' Massa is kind, and compassionate."

This from a man who as a teenager, had tried to *murder* his mother—with a hammer?

Damn!

House Negro Hershel Walker…!

"What I like to do is see it and everything and stuff."

This was Hershel Walker's response, when asked about gun control, after the killing of 21 people at a school in Uvalde Texas.

And what does he think about climate change?

"Since we don't control the air, our good air decided to float over to China's bad air so when China gets our good air, their bad air got to move. So it moves over to our good air space. Then now we got to clean that back up, while they're messing ours up."

And what does he think about the Inflation Reduction Act?

"The Inflation Reduction Act doesn't help Americans, because of lot of money it's going to trees. And we have enough trees"

When Donald Trump searched high and low, for a Plantation House Negro, to endorse in the 2022 GOP senate race in Georgia, someone who was as *clear*-headed, and as intelligent, as he was, someone whose problem-solving ideas were as *lucid* and as keenly focused, as his were, he thought long and hard—for a long, long second, or two—and said, "*Eenie… meenie… miney… mo*," then kissed himself, and flicked his pinky at Hershel.

Hershel and Donald were old pals dating back to Trump's failed attempt to establish the CFL Football League, a sock it to the jaw of the National Football League that had spurn his bid to buy a major league team.

The two remained close friends over the decades, and recently, when asked if Trump had repeatedly falsely stated that the 2020 Presidential election was *stolen*, he said:

"I think reporters said that. I don't know whether President Trump said that. He's never said that to me… I'm not saying the president, but everyone knows that something happened in the election. Do you know what happened? I think something happened. I don't know what it was—but something happened—because people are angry. Guys, there's people that they're *unhappy*, with the election. Do you know what happened? I think something happened. I don't know *what* it was—but *something* happened—because people… are *angry*."

Like his mentor—and Massa—Trump—he also believes that there are miracle cures that could stop the Covid-19 virus in its tracks, but no one wants to talk about it. In a Glenn Beck interview, he said that he had a dry mist that could clean anyone from the Covid virus, and it was FDA approved. He went on to say that, "I *shouldn't* tell any-one… but… I *have* something that [can be brought] into a building, that will clean you of COVID, as you walk through this, this dry mist. When you leave, it will *kill* the virus…!"

Hershel, a Black sheep-herder in his spare time, seems to be on a mission that will not just deliver his flock to the old auction-block, but deliver them *dead*, on arrival, at the old auction-black.

House Negro Senator Tim Scott…!

"Some of the generals just give me a dime and didn't say nothin' but they wasn't big men like General Lee. He was straight and dignified and didn't talk much, but he'd walk up and down on the front gallery and the orderlies brung him telegraphs from Bull Run. I heard them talkin 'bout 'Bull Run' that day and I [thought]

somebody's bull had got out and us and the Yankees was tryin' to ketch him and git him back in the pasture."

—Frank Smith, former slave, interviewed in the 1930s by the WPA.

Some members of the Republican Party just give Tim Scott a dime, but they ain't big men, like his oval-headed orange-colored leader who gives him a *whole* dollar.

Tim Scott, the lone Black Republican senator in the entire U.S. Senate, has this to say about his life as a Black man in America:

"While I thank *God!* I have not endured bodily harm, I have, however, felt the pressure applied by the scales of justice when they are slanted. I have *felt* the anger, the *frustration*, the *sadness* and the *humiliation* that comes with feeling like you're being targeted for nothing more than being just yourself."

But like most Republicans he sees no evil, hears no evil, and speaks no evil, when the subject turns to his party's racist attack on voting rights, and other issues that directly affect Blacks and minorities in his own district.

He *saw* no evil, *heard,* no evil, and *spoke,* no evil, at Trump's impeachment hearings, when witness after witness described in stunning details how *his* President had not only participated in a failed coup attempt against his *own* country, but had orchestrated, a failed coup attempt, against his *own* country; and he saw no evil, heard, no evil, and spoke, no evil, when *his* President said that African countries are shithole countries, or when he questioned whether President Obama had the right to call himself an American citizen.

Referring to the January 6 coup attempt, and who should be held responsible, he says, "The one person I don't blame, is [my teacher, and long-time lover] President *Trump!*"

More recently, not a single Republican senator supported a bill that would have fought the *violent* actions of white supremacists, including, Tim Scott, his Black constituents' *best* friend—and ally.

Sprouting the same old *pull yourself up by your own bootless bootstraps* sprouted by his Republican partners in insanity, he seems to be exactly the kind of politician that Malcomb X warned us about, when he said:

"Negro leaders are not really Negro leaders. These are puppets that have been put in front of the Negro community. These are parrots..."

House Negro Allen West...!

Allen West, a retired Army Lieutenant, and a Tea-Party supported member of the Republican Party, was born on February 7 in 1961.

West was elected to the Florida House of Representatives' 22nd congressional district in 2010, becoming the first Black man to occupy that position since Joshua T. Wells left office in 1876.

But comparing West, to Joshua Wells, is like comparing tomatoes to apples, and daylight to *storming* night.

Joshua Wells born a slave in 1842, was forced to fight for the Confederacy during the Civil War, and was captured by the Union Army where he quickly switched sides and joined the U.S. Colored Troops in 1863, rising to the rank of corporal. As Florida's first Black congressman Walls introduced bills to establish education funding and aid to Seminole War Veterans, whereas West, in the same position, offended veterans' groups by comparing Social Security disability benefits, to slavery.

Today, West sees himself as a modern-day Harriet Tubman, ferrying wailing black souls from the bondage of liberal-handout-Democrats, to the sink-or-swim-do-or-die-*screw*-you—up-one-side and-down-another—right-wing *extremism*, espoused by he and his fellow Republicans.

He called Obama an abject failure: and a socialist agitator.

"I believe the election and reelection of Obama were among the most conspicuous acts of denial in recent years. Voters just stopped paying attention!"

And holding no punches he threw a round-house uppercut to the jaw of the first Black president, and his followers, when he said that drivers with Obama stickers, are "a *threat* to the gene-pool!"

And what does he think of Donald Trump, his bosom Negro hating buddy, who has done more for the Black race than anyone—with the possible exception of Abraham Lincoln?

"I've got the message up to him," West told a reporter. "I'd *like* to see the president come *back* to Texas one more time, especially come back to North Texas [and help us overthrow this election]!"

After the Supreme Court dismissed a lawsuit seeking to overturn the 2020 election and declare Donald Trump the winner, he said that the unfair judgement calls for drastic *actions!*

Calling for the return of slavery, he said: "Perhaps law-abiding states should bond together and form a Union of states, which will abide by the [Confederate} constitution," suggesting that once again the time had come… to *secede*… from *tyranny!*

And what does Trump think of his present-day Harriet Tubman, in drag?

In a tweet *applauding* Allen, for herding Ol' Massa's Negroes *back* to the Old Homestead, the President tweeted:

"Congratulations Allen, great job!"

House Negroes Diamond and Silk…!

Lynnette Hardaway and Rochelle Richardson—Diamond and Silk—right wing political activists, and Fox TV commentators, have called Nancy Pelosi a non-functioning alcoholic, has said that Donald Trump would *work* for the people, that he was *concerned* about the American worker, and that those who voted for Obama don't have enough change to buy a loaf of bread. "We want a government that works for the [white] people, not against the [white] people. That's why *we* are [House Negro] Trump *supporters!*"

House Negro Ali Alexander...!

"I'm the guy who came up with the idea of January 6 when I was talking with Congressman Gosar, Congressman Andy Biggs, and Congressman Mo Brooks. So we're the four guys who came up with a January 6 [insurrection] event..."

His rationale, for his insurrection-inspiring idea?

Alexander says he merely wanted to convince [Vice President Pence], "to not certify the vote on January 6, and close that city down!"

But when five people were killed in a riot that *he* instigated, he said, sheepishly, "*Me...?*"

Alexander, who endeared himself to President Trump by tweeting that Kamala Harris was not a Black American, says that he needs $2,000 a day to fund his security detail and other expenses (while he remains in hiding) and will gladly accept donations from his fans.

The on-the-run Trump loyalist, one of the President's most *intelligent* fans, says that he is not only being hounded by law enforcement officials, but he believes that he is being targeted by the *supernatural*. "Witches and wiccans! are putting hexes, and *curses* on us!"

He explained.

House Negro Pastor Mark Burns...!

He calls Donald Trump a *smart* man. And he thinks that Trump recognizes *real* character [like his].

After the storming of the U.S. Capitol on January 2021 by Trump supporters, Burns was among those who advanced the conspiracy theory that people associated with Antifa were responsible for the attack.

Calling himself "Trump's Favorite [House Negro] Pastor, he spends weekends at the president's plush Mara-a-Lago Club in Florida, paling around with members of the president's family and inner circle.

"When people say Donald Trump is a racist, I *know* what racism looks like, OK?" he preaches. "And it *ain't!* [my Negro-hanging, Massa] *Trump!*"

When his master is sick, the modern-day House Negro says: "What the matter, boss, we sick?" And if you ask the modern-day House Negro to work together, to get ahead, he will point his gun at your head and ask: "Are you are *cra-zy!*" Where can I eat better food than this? Where can I wear better clothes than this? And he will tell you that: "I's is gonna be a good *nigger*, till I *die!*"

An old African Proverb:

"If there is no enemy inside the house, the enemy outside the house, can do no harm."

From the movie, Trading Places:

Restroom scene: Eddie Murphy, in the role of a Black former street hustler who naïvely thinks that he has made a success of himself on Wall Street, is in the restroom of a very prestigious trading firm, smoking a cigarette in a bathroom-stall. He ducks and hides inside the stall as his white, stiff-necked bosses barges into the restroom suddenly. Inside the stall, Eddie Murphy in the role of Valentine listens intently, as his two bosses settle a little wager they had made at the beginning of the movie.

Randolph: Pay up Mortimer, I've won the bet.

Mortimer: Here. One dollar.

Randolph: We took a perfectly useless psychopath, like Valentine, and turned him into a successful executive. During the same time, we turned an honest hardworking man, into a violently deranged, would-be killer... Now, what are we going to do about taking [his nephew] Winthrope back, and turning Valentine to the ghetto?

Mortimer: I don't want Winthrope back, after what he's done.

Randolph: You mean, keep Valentine on as managing director?

Mortimer: Do you really believe I would have a Nigger running our family business, Randolph?

Randolph: Of course not. Neither would I. I do think we should hold off on switching them back, though, till we get that crop report on New Year's Eve, don't you?

Mortimer: Absolutely. No sense rocking the boat until then.

Randolph: If Mister Beach does what we paid him to do, we should have a very happy New Year.

Mortimer: In-de-e-d.

As the two Wall Street blue-bloods laughs and strides triumphantly out of the bathroom, Valentine, inside the stall, has the dazed look of a Negro who finally knows the score: A Negro, who at long last realizes, that no matter how high he rises in the service of the Massa's boys on Wall Street, he is and will remain, just another twenty-first century Negro, on somebody's new, but very *old*, plantation.

Chapter Twelve
The Back to the Plantation Trump Era

Oh *please* Mister Trump… I don't wanna go…

There's a big war! In the streets!

Fear in every-one I meet,

Tanks attacking the Immigrants,

Rockets blasting the Government,

White Nationalists running wild,

The KKK is back in style,

Big buildings along the tracks,

Are piling up bodies in tall stacks,

My bags are packed and I'm going away,

Because I'm Black! I must pay!

So please Mister Trump… I don't wanna go…

There's a gas-oven waitin' out there!

Just itchin' to scorch my hair!

Now there's a knock, at my door,

Soldiers say it's time to go,

Oh, *please*, Mis-ter Trump!

Please, please, *please*… Master Trump…!

Can you spare this old, very tired, old, Negro…?

"In the year 1886, Henry Grady, an editor of the Atlanta Constitution, had spoken at a dinner in New York. In the audience were J. P. Morgan, H. M. Flagler (an associate of Rockefeller), Russell Sage, and Charles Tiffany. His talk was called 'The New

South' and his theme was: Let bygones be bygones; let us have a new era of peace and prosperity; the Negro was a prosperous laboring class; he had the fullest protection of the laws and the friendship of the southern people. Grady joked about the northerners who had sold slaves to the South, and said the South could now handle its own race problem. He received a rising ovation, and the band played 'Dixie'."

—Horace Mann Bond.

In the Trump era of governance, licking your finger, and holding it to the wind, you would not have felt the chilliness in the air the former slaves experienced soon after slavery, you would have felt cold, numbing, icicles, swirling from the North Pole.

In the Trump era of governance, and in the era of the here and now: the Southern Elites, and Northern Elites, and the Eastern and the Western Elites—letting bygones be bygones—and following the lead of their Dear Leader, have decreed, by their actions, that the sub-human Negro should forever be the sub-human he was meant to be. And should be treated, accordingly.

And if one listens, *listens* closely, the twanging banjo sound of Dixie can very distinctly be heard, *drifting*, in the foggy background: And one is left to ponder: is it merely a coincidence that that Big Chill in the air seems once again to be drifting from that odiously, *Southerly*, direction?

And with Census Reports stating that whites will soon become the minority, and the minorities the majority (with white dominance, and white supremacy under attack) one is left to ponder, also, if the time has come… to let those bygones, do their dance?

After all: The modern-day Negro has been a prosperous laboring class, he has had the *fullest* protection of the laws and the *friendship* of all of the American people.

But… has the boy strayed… a bit too far, from his *lowly*, origins…?

And now, another question, arises: Have the *Big* Boys moving the money placed their bets on their own uninterested white interests; and decided that, unfortunately, the interests of the hated Negro, and those hated like him, *has to* go…

Back? All the way back? *Back* to the back of the bus?

Back?

Back to Ozzie and Harriet, and Leave It to Beaver, and the sweet acrid smell of Negroes *roasting* on an open pit; back, to the glory days of high-jumping from low-pumping bullets, all-l the *way* back, back to the golden days when America truly *was* the land of the *free* and the *home*… (yuk!) of the *brave*…?

Thumbing through the pages of history we see where the South always said it would rise again.

And under the Trump era: Rise, it has: To the tune of Dixie, and Tote That Barge, and Lift That Bale, and Get A Little Drunk You Gonna Land In Jail, the South, and the *real* America, is back, and on the *prowl*.

With an Orange Haired Tin-Horn Russian Loving Dictator screaming the Rebel Yell and leading the charge on a witch's broomstick, the tattered boys in gray have armed themselves: for The Great Reckoning; when Lee flanked by the Sons of the Confederacy will rise from the ashes, to smite the Mexicans, and the Muslims, and the Jews, and the Darkies (no country in its right mind could be this damned *crazy!* could it?).

Yes… that *coldness*, in the air, the former slave experienced soon after slavery, has once again crept into the nation's conscience.

And America appears to have reached that time in history, when the Old Master's Old Guard is on the ropes; as it tries desperately to remain relevant in a changing world that it fears, and despises.

On the ropes and fearing the knockout punch it has feared since Colonial Times, the white ruling class seems to have reached a critical life or death cross-roads. Battling a rebellious Black race that has gotten a fairly good taste of freedom, and facing the very real possibility that all of their book banning activities will fail, and all of their voter suppressions bills will fail, and all of their fear campaigns will fail; where do they go, from that point on?

To the streets, in an open revolt?

White supremacists [conducted] a reign of terror throughout the South. White Southerners from all classes of society joined the Klan's ranks, in the name of preserving law and order... They whipped the teachers of freedmen's schools and burnt their schoolhouses.

—PBS, Grant, Reconstruction, and the KKK.

When a very loud and vocal minority is firmly convinced that America is *their* land, and their land, *only*, can we be but a heartbeat away from that violence that began shortly after the Civil War?

And does this mean, that the *real* America is back in the saddle, on a fast galloping ride back to the glory days Ozzie and Harriet and Leave It To Beaver, and the sweet acrid smell of Negroes burning on a charred rope?

Sadly, the *real* America after a brief hiatus appears once again to be back—on a midnight round-up of all its undesirables?

The *real* America, the America that the Founding Fathers envisioned... is *back?*

Chapter Thirteen
Chained to the Old Plantation

In the final analysis: when we see that the Black man has been ambushed from all directions for more than 150 years, when we see that slavery, Jim Crow, Cointelpro, the crack-cocaine epidemic, the Thug Rap epidemic, white apathy, Black apathy, social engineering, unjust punitive laws, and just plain old black human nature and plain old white human nature has played, in the overall equation as well, we are then left to conclude that we should not ask for whom that great Bell of Guilt tolls; we see that it tolls for All Of Us!

Yes, it seems that every-one, and the *snake* they rode in on, have had a ravenous unquenchable taste for Black meat... even Plantation House—ho'—Negroes, find it to be a *strange*, but *tasty*...? delicacy...?

Yes, it seems that everyone—and, the *bed bug* they hitched a ride on—has had their teeth gum deep in one part or another of the tattered Black man's anatomy, since the first slave stepped off the boat with a bewildered this can't be happening look on his searching for an exit face.

And with so many mouths feasting so happily on so many parts of his anatomy, for so many tiring, gruesome years, and centuries, the question is not *how is it* that the Black man has not moved one iota from the old plantation, the question is, how in hellish America, could he manage to *move* a damned *muscle*! His ability to stay afloat in the fierce smoke-filled battle—ambushed from all sides—including the Homefront—should not be criticized, but celebrated: as one of the greatest, most heroic achievements, of *all* times!

****

"White folks, you can have your automobiles and paved streets and electric lights. I don't want 'em. You can have the buses and street cars and hot pavements and high buildings 'cause I ain't got no use for 'em no way. But I'll tell you what I does want. I wants my old cotton bed and the moonlight nights a shinin' through the willow trees and the cool grass under my feet as I run around catching lightnin' bugs. I wants to hear the sound of the hounds in the woods after the 'possum, and the smell of fresh mowed hay. I wants to feel the sway of the ol' wagon a-goin' down the red, dusty road and listen to the wheels groanin' as they rolls along. I wants to sink my teeth into some of that good ol' ash cake, and smack the good ol' sorghum off my mouth. White folks... I wants to see the dawn break over the black ridge and the twilight settle over the place spreadin' a sort of orange hue... I wants to walk the paths through the woods and see the rabbits and watch the birds and listen to frogs at night... But

they took me away from that a long time ago… Now I just live from hand to mouth; here one day, somewhere else the next. Maybe someday I'll git to go home… They tells me that when a person crosses that river, the Lord gives him what he wants. I done told the Lord I don't want nothin' much. Only my home, white folks. I don't think that's much to ask for. I supposed he'll send me back there. I been waitin…"

—Clara Davis, former slave.

Miss Clara.

When you look down and see the fruit that your toil has reaped, do you turn away?

And when you *gaze* upon that twilight spreading across the fields, in that deep orange hue that you recall so lovingly, and see the *plight* of your liberated children; do you fall… to your *knees?*

Is the rain… *your* tears?

www.ingramcontent.com/pod-product-compliance
Lightning Source LLC
Chambersburg PA
CBHW050340160726

48002CB00001B/387